Brian Urlacher

FOOTBALL SUPERSTARS

Tiki Barber

Tom Brady

Reggie Bush

John Elway

Brett Favre

Eli Manning

Peyton Manning

Dan Marino

Donovan McNabb

Joe Montana

Walter Payton

Adrian Peterson

Jerry Rice

Ben Roethlisberger

Tony Romo

Barry Sanders

LaDainian Tomlinson

Brian Urlacher

FOOTBALL ● SUPERSTARS

Brian Urlacher

Jon Sterngass

CHELSEA HOUSE
An Infobase Learning Company

BRIAN URLACHER

Chelsea House
An imprint of Infobase Learning
132 West 31st Street
New York, NY 10001

Library of Congress Cataloging-in-Publication Data
Sterngass, Jon.
  Brian Urlacher / by Jon Sterngass.
     p. cm. — (Football superstars)
  Includes bibliographical references and index.
  ISBN 978-1-60413-752-1 (hardcover)
  1. Urlacher, Brian—Juvenile literature. 2. Football players—United States—Biography—Juvenile literature. I. Title.
  GV939.U76S84 2011
  796.332092—dc22
  [B]
                              2011004490

Chelsea House books are available at special discounts when purchased in bulk quantities for businesses, associations, institutions, or sales promotions. Please call our Special Sales Department in New York at (212) 967-8800 or (800) 322-8755.

You can find Chelsea House on the World Wide Web at http://www.infobaselearning.com

Text design by Erik Lindstrom
Cover design by Ben Peterson and Keith Trego
Composition by EJB Publishing Services
Cover printed by Bang Printing, Brainerd, Mn.
Book printed and bound by Bang Printing, Brainerd, Mn.
Date printed: October 2011
Printed in the United States of America

10 9 8 7 6 5 4 3 2 1

This book is printed on acid-free paper.

All links and Web addresses were checked and verified to be correct at the time of publication. Because of the dynamic nature of the Web, some addresses and links may have changed since publication and may no longer be valid.

CONTENTS

Most Overrated?

When Brian Urlacher was named the National Football League (NFL) Defensive Rookie of the Year in 2000 and the NFL Defensive Player of the Year in 2005, he became only the fifth player in NFL history to win both awards. Yet despite his achievements on the field, many people still found a great deal to criticize. Some detractors cited his lack of ability to take on blocks. A writer for the *Chicago Sun-Times* called him the NFL's most overrated player. When the 2006 season began, analysts noted that Urlacher had never won a play-off game.

In October 2006, a controversial *Sports Illustrated* poll of 361 NFL players voted Urlacher the second-most overrated player in the NFL behind Terrell Owens. Urlacher garnered 8 percent of the vote, which equated to about 29 players.

Reporters asked Urlacher about the poll on October 29 after Chicago had won its seventh straight game by crushing the San Francisco 49ers 41-10. Urlacher gave the only possible answer; he said that how he performed on the field would answer his critics. "Just watch the film," Urlacher said. "All I can do is go out there and play hard and try and help my team win, and that's what I'm going to keep doing."

The film of the San Francisco game was revealing. On a first-quarter blitz, Urlacher deflected a pass up in the air and then made an amazing interception with one hand while falling to the ground with a 300-pound (136-kilogram) San Francisco guard draped all over him. Chicago's defensive coordinator, Ron Rivera, said that Urlacher's catch was the type of phenomenal play that just could not be coached. "It's just being aware— great ball awareness, great athletic ability, and just tremendous effort by him," Rivera said. "And with his attitude and spirit, he's going to make plays like that." That very season, Urlacher would lead the Bears to Super Bowl XLI, their first appearance in the championship game since 1985.

FAN FAVORITE

By the start of the 2011 season, Urlacher had amassed 1,160 tackles, 41.5 sacks, and 18 interceptions while being selected to seven career Pro Bowls. ESPN named him to their All-Decade team in 2009. "At his best," ESPN wrote, "the 260-pound [118-kilogram] Urlacher was athletic enough to play the deep middle in coverage, yet strong enough to punish receivers and running backs on underneath plays."

How is it possible that someone with Urlacher's career accomplishments could be overrated? Perhaps the answer is that Urlacher is more than just a great middle linebacker. For a decade, he has been the symbol of the Chicago Bears. Most NFL teams promote and glorify offensive players like quarterbacks and running backs. In Chicago, Urlacher, a defensive player, is the main star and the face of the franchise. He is almost worshipped by many of the fans who flock to Soldier Field wearing a jersey or T-shirt with his name on it. Years of ceaseless promotion have led to an inevitable backlash.

THE POLL

An October 2006 *Sports Illustrated* poll asked 361 NFL players, "Who is the NFL's most overrated player?" The results raised a few eyebrows. Bears linebacker Brian Urlacher was voted second-most overrated, but he was in good company. Linebacker Ray Lewis was a two-time Defensive Player of the Year. Warren Sapp went to the Pro Bowl seven times as a defensive tackle, and Charles Woodson went five times as a cornerback. Quarterbacks Peyton Manning, Eli Manning, and Ben Roethlisberger would all lead their teams to Super Bowl victories. Terrell Owens has 153 receiving touchdowns (as of 2011), second all-time in the NFL. The list seemed to reflect the resentment that many NFL players felt toward the star-making machinery of the league and the media rather than a judgment on the players named.

Here are the results of the poll (showing players with their 2006 teams):

Terrell Owens	Cowboys	10 percent
Brian Urlacher	Bears	8 percent
Ray Lewis	Ravens	7 percent
Michael Vick	Falcons	7 percent
Eli Manning	Giants	4 percent
Keyshawn Johnson	Panthers	4 percent
Peyton Manning	Colts	4 percent
Ben Roethlisberger	Steelers	3 percent
Charles Woodson	Packers	3 percent
Warren Sapp	Raiders	3 percent

Almost as soon as he joined the Bears in 2000, Urlacher became a fan favorite in Chicago. Bears supporters loved the way he closed on a runner or a receiver with his unbelievable speed, slammed him to the ground, and then grinned as he offered a hand to help him up. Urlacher's popularity turned him into as big a force in the marketing arena as he was on the playing field.

In 2002, the Urlacher No. 54 replica jersey was the most popular seller in the NFL, and it has remained one of the biggest sellers for the rest of his career. "We can't keep them in stock," said Carol Langan, the manager of a sports and novelty store in downtown Chicago. "The authentic jersey costs $200. They come in and buy it without the blink of an eye—two or three times a day." Urlacher jerseys flooded Chicago. "It's just exciting to see all those '54' jerseys out there in the stands," Urlacher said. "It's crazy how people have taken to me."

Urlacher claimed that he did not seek the spotlight and felt uncomfortable doing advertisements. "I just don't like calling attention to myself," he told one reporter. "It's a team sport. I think I've always been brought up to be a humble person, knowing that I can still do things better." There was never any reason to doubt his sincerity.

In his desire to make money from advertisements, however, he seemed to be everywhere to the point of overexposure. He had advertising contracts with Nike, Vitamin Water, Ace Hardware, and AT&T Home Turf. Television viewers saw him on commercials for Campbell's Soup, Old Spice, Domino's Pizza, McDonald's, and MasterCard. He was on the cover of SEGA Sports NFL, and Urlacher bobbleheads were best sellers in Chicago. His picture appeared in every major sports magazine, and he was quoted in countless newspaper and television stories. "He's very quickly becoming like a god in this city," Jay Mariotti, a local sportswriter, marveled.

Urlacher's small-town New Mexico upbringing, his rise to prominence "out of nowhere," and his understated attitude on the field appealed especially to the midwestern Chicago fans. His easygoing attitude made him extremely marketable in Chicago and throughout the NFL. It was only natural that some NFL players not as fortunately positioned, as well as some football analysts resentful of the unending hype, would decide that Urlacher was overrated.

PART OF THE PANTHEON?

How important are postseason accomplishments? The Chicago Bears' Dick Butkus, who played from 1965 to 1973, is widely considered the best middle linebacker of all time. Many people consider his teammate Gale Sayers (1965–1971) the best open-field runner ever. Yet the Bears were mediocre in those years (48–74–4 from 1965 to 1973), and neither superstar ever played in a single postseason game. Should that fact figure into an evaluation of their overall accomplishments?

As of 2011, Urlacher's Bears are 3–4 in the postseason and have played in Super Bowl XLI. (The Bears did not win it, however.) "I want to be remembered as a championship football player," Urlacher said. "But I don't think that, if you don't [win the Super Bowl], you've failed in your career. We've done some good things since I've been here."

None of the media promotion could take away from the fact that Urlacher was a superb football player. His supporters argued that it was not fair to judge him based on the hype he did not create. Instead, all that should count was his performance on the field. That performance, whether measured statistically, by team achievement, or by honors, was quite impressive.

As the Bears' middle linebacker, Urlacher was 6-foot-4 (1.93 meters) and 260 pounds (118 kilograms), with unearthly 4.6-second speed for the 40-yard (36.5-meter) dash. From a town of 10,000 people in New Mexico, Urlacher led his high school to a state championship. He received only two scholarship offers but managed to lead the entire NCAA in tackles as a safety at the University of New Mexico. Chosen by the Chicago

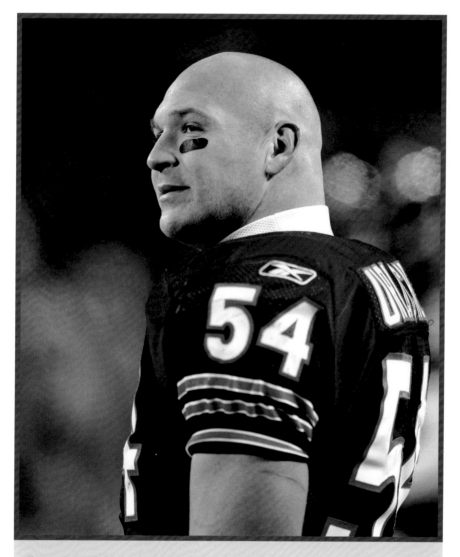

Chicago Bears' defensive linebacker Brian Urlacher is considered one of the best players in the NFL. Some believe he's one of the most overrated. Urlacher, who has been selected to seven Pro Bowls, believes that his performance on the field speaks for itself.

Bears as the ninth pick in the NFL Draft in 2000, he surprised everyone by winning Defensive Rookie of the Year honors.

Since then, Urlacher has been a steady force in his years with the Bears. He recorded more than 100 tackles in seven of his first eight seasons. In all seven of those years, Urlacher led the Bears in tackles. The only exception was the 2004 season, when injuries prevented him from playing in seven games.

Urlacher had at least four especially great seasons. In 2001, Urlacher led the Bears to the play-offs with 116 tackles and won the *Football Digest* NFL Defensive Player of the Year award. The next year, he had a career-high 151 tackles, the most ever by a Bear since the NFL began recording tackles in 1971.

In 2005, Urlacher led his team to the play-offs again with 121 tackles. For his efforts, he won the Associated Press Defensive Player of the Year award, the highest honor an NFL defensive player can achieve. In 2001 and 2005, Urlacher was the main reason that Chicago allowed the fewest points in the entire NFL. In 2005, the Bears allowed only 202 points in 16 games. The next year, he was the driving force behind the Bears' 13–3 season and their appearance in Super Bowl XLI.

A *pantheon* is a list of all the gods of a particular religion or mythology. Chicago is a football town, and the city's mythology revolves around the fortunes of the Bears. Since the 1950s, Chicago's hard-hitting middle linebackers have defined the team's identity: Bill George, Dick Butkus, and Mike Singletary. All three were NFL Hall of Famers and among the best middle linebackers of all time. Does Brian Urlacher belong with these immortals?

Let's take Urlacher's advice. We can't "look at the film," but we can look back on his life and football career. Then we can judge if Urlacher deserves to join the pantheon of Chicago's middle linebacker demigods.

Early Years

Brian Keith Urlacher was born in Pasco, Washington, on May 25, 1978, to parents Lavoyda and Brad Urlacher. He was a middle child; Sheri was his older sister by a year, and Casey was born 15 months later in 1979. Brian was a plump 11-pound, 8-ounce (5.2-kilogram) baby. Lavoyda Urlacher remembered, "The doctor told me right then, 'You have a football player on your hands.'"

Lavoyda was only 16 when she married her high school boyfriend, and she had the three children by the time she was 19. The marriage did not last, however, and Lavoyda was divorced by age 25. In 1986, she moved with her children to Lovington, New Mexico, where her family lived. At the time, Brian was eight years old and in second grade.

Lavoyda juggled jobs at a laundry, a grocery store, and a convenience store to make ends meet. Sometimes, the children spent more time with their babysitters than with their mother. "We ate a lot of macaroni and cheese during that time," she said, "but the kids never went without. I had energy and desire, and I swore we were going to make it one way or another."

Six years after the family moved to Lovington, Lavoyda married Troy Lenard, a part-time cowboy and full-time pipeliner in the local oil fields. Lenard's discipline helped add structure that the family needed. "Brian didn't have much as a kid," Brandon Ridenour, one of Brian's childhood friends, said. "His family lived paycheck to paycheck. Every role model he had has been a hardworking type." Brian once said, "My mom is my heart, but my [step]dad was my role model, the hardest working man I ever knew."

Urlacher respected his stepfather. "You know, going up in the oil fields, seeing everyone work [there]. . . . My [stepfather] was at work at five in the morning every day. I saw that growing up. That was just the No. 1 thing, just the work ethic." Brian's biological father, Brad Urlacher, stayed in Washington, and Brian had almost no contact with him. "I guess it's good to have a relationship with him," Brian said, "but he'll never be considered my real dad as far as I'm concerned." Urlacher considered Troy Lenard his "real dad."

As a kid, Brian was especially close to Casey, his younger brother. The boys shared a room with Lenard's son, David, and the three of them had good times growing up together. Brian and Casey were so competitive that they refused to play baseball on the same team. Brian remembered one incident when "I was pitching and the first time he came up, Casey took me to the fence. Absolutely knocked the crap out of the ball. So the next time up, naturally, I had to bean him. We were always

Urlacher (*second from left*) grew up in a competitive family with hardworking role models. Above, older sister Sheri (*left*) and younger brother Casey (*right*) join Urlacher and his wife, Laurie (*second from right*), in their hometown high school for a ceremony honoring his achievements.

competitive, always wanted to be better than the other guy. We didn't realize how lucky we were to be together."

17,000 OIL RIGS

The place where people grow up influences their character and life choices, and Brian Urlacher was no exception. "I've been brought up that if you want to get something, you're going to have to work for it," Urlacher said. "There's no other way to get it. No one's going to give you anything. That's just the way I live my life." These values partially came from growing up in Lovington, New Mexico, a small town of about 10,000 people. It is tucked in the southeast corner of the state, about 20 miles

(32 kilometers) from the west Texas border. It is so isolated that the nearest major airport is 110 miles (177 kilometers) northeast in Lubbock, Texas.

Lovington is barely more than a few traffic lights surrounded by ranch and farmland and about 17,000 oil rigs. The oil wells date from the 1950s when the Denton oil pool was discovered about nine miles (14 kilometers) northeast of Lovington. The oil industry shaped the economy, labor force, and lifestyle of Lovington. About 2,000 people were living in the town in 1940, but the population increased 500 percent between 1940 and 1960 because of the oil industry. Growth has stagnated since then, and the town has become an oilfield backwater. Just about the only other jobs stem from Lovington's position as the county seat of Lea County. The total population of Lea County could barely fill an average NFL stadium on a Sunday afternoon in the fall.

Opportunities for culture or social life were limited in Lovington. The town was famous in rodeo circles for producing seven world champion calf and team ropers. In general, however, life revolved around the oil wells and the football field. "Here," one teenager, Chantz Clayton, said, "you play football or watch people play football. There's nothing else to do." Since it is so close to Texas, Lovington shared its *Friday Night Lights* culture of high school football. The high school stadium held 6,000 people and was usually full Friday nights during the season.

HIGH SCHOOL CAREER

Because there was not much else to do in Lovington, the Urlacher boys naturally drifted into sports. "We played street football and played basketball, ran track, played baseball, all that good stuff," Urlacher said. He loved football, but he did not particularly excel at it when he was younger. "He was just an average freshman," Jaime Quiñones, his assistant coach, said. "Nothing to indicate what the future would be like."

As a sophomore at Lovington High School, Urlacher was about 5-foot-9 (1.75 meters) and 150 pounds (68 kilograms). He played wide receiver on the football team, and his coach Speedy Faith noted, "He wasn't the most gifted receiver we had," but he was willing to work extremely hard. By the end of the season, he had gained the attention of one of the assistant coaches, who urged him to hit the weights in the off-season if he wanted to go anywhere in football.

Brian and Casey lifted early (5:30 A.M.) and often (four times a week). Quiñones noted, "He had a tremendous work ethic. . . . He worked out every morning, even in the off-season when it wasn't mandatory." Brian was driven. He would tell people, "I'm going to play for the Dallas Cowboys some day."

The hard work paid off when the Urlacher boys began to grow. By Brian's senior year in high school, he stood 6-foot-4 (1.93 meters) and weighed 210 pounds (95 kilograms). Yet with his size and strength, he maintained his speed. The combination made him a standout for Lovington High School, and he became a legend in the dusty New Mexico town. Years later, one resident vividly recalled Urlacher's feats on the football field: "He was the best football player I ever saw. He made plays I still have in my mind."

A FOOTBALL POWERHOUSE

The Lovington High School Wildcats are a football powerhouse in Class 3A in New Mexico. The team is a great source of pride to the local community. When Brian Urlacher started high school in 1992, the team had won 11 state championships (17 as of 2011), the second most in New Mexico.

In his senior year, Urlacher was New Mexico's best player and was named an all-state wide receiver and safety. He was so big and so fast that he played both offense and defense. "We were smart enough to get him the ball any way possible," Faith said. He was the team's leading tackler and caught 61 passes for 15 touchdowns. He scored eight more touchdowns on four punt returns, two kickoff returns, and two rushing touchdowns. He set school records for most points in a season (142), most touchdowns in a season (23), most receiving yards in a game (194), and most total yards in a season (1,348).

"On offense, our philosophy was just to get the ball to him," Quiñones said. "You could just throw it up, and he'd jump and dominate." Brian, however, preferred to be on the other side of the line of scrimmage. "I played a lot of offense," he said. "But I liked defense better. Rather hit than get hit. I was always right on the edge of being legal. If you were standing around the pile, I'd crush you."

As a senior in 1995, Urlacher led the team to an undefeated 14–0 season, the Class 3A New Mexico championship, and a No. 10 national ranking in the *USA Today* high school football poll. His brother Casey, a sophomore, was the team's defensive end. "If Casey didn't hit people at the line of scrimmage," Brian later remembered, "I hit them right afterwards."

Brian was an extremely clutch player. "He was a man among boys in big games," Quiñones said. "If you threw it to him, he would catch it. If you kicked it to him, he'd return it. If you tried to throw a pass at him, he'd intercept it."

In the Class 3A state championship game, Lovington was locked in a difficult battle with Silver High School. Urlacher caught seven passes for 107 yards and two touchdowns, while intercepting two passes and forcing two fumbles on defense. One of his plays, an amazing leaping interception, turned the game around and has become a New Mexico legend.

"I FELT LUCKY"

"How could I get in trouble in Lovington?" Urlacher said. "We played Ping-Pong in guys' garages all night; we'd cruise the strip drinking chocolate milk. And we'd play sports." Urlacher and his best friend made a pact never to drink alcohol in high school. By all accounts, they kept their pledge, not an easy job in an isolated town of 10,000. "Brian always made curfew back then; he was the solid one," Troy Lenard said. "But, now, Casey and David, they were just downright mean and ornery." Lavoyda Urlacher claimed that Brian always displayed strong character and upstanding behavior. "He was never in trouble," she said. "He always made good grades, and I just never had any problems with him at all. If I told him to be home by 10 o'clock, he was home at 10 o'clock."

When he was not playing football, Brian was an all-district basketball player. He had a 38-inch (97-centimeter) vertical leap and averaged 25 points and 15 rebounds his senior season. Ping-Pong, though, was his side passion. He never tired of playing, and he loved to win. "He's a Ping-Pong fanatic," one friend, Scott Karger, said. "He'll try to beat you 21-0. He doesn't care." He would keep that passion into adulthood. "He has his own paddle and he carries it around in his car in case he needs it," friend Brandon Ridenour marveled. "He's convinced he's the best Ping-Pong player in the world."

As a senior, Brian was just hoping to play college football anywhere. Because he was small as a sophomore, recruiters did not notice him early. However, when Brian became a dominating force as a senior, he still did not attract much attention. Although he was an all-state wide receiver and defensive back, the state was New Mexico, generally thought of as a football backwater.

Urlacher dreamed of attending Texas Tech just across the border in nearby Lubbock. Texas Tech was a major Division I power and regularly went to postseason bowl games. Zach Thomas, an All-Pro linebacker in the NFL, had graduated from the school in 1995.

Unlike other high school football stars, Urlacher was not offered many scholarships. Shut out of Texas Tech, his first choice, he accepted a football scholarship at the University of New Mexico.

Texas Tech, however, was not interested in Brian. The coaches there told him only that he was welcome to try to make the team as a walk-on. In fact, the only college to show interest was the University of New Mexico (UNM). After UNM offered him a scholarship, New Mexico State, another Division I school, also offered a scholarship. And that was it—two scholarship offers for the future NFL Defensive Player of the Year.

Urlacher chose to play for New Mexico and coach Dennis Franchione over New Mexico State. Quiñones later said, "It was a godsend that Tech neglected him. New Mexico was a perfect fit."

The summer after his senior year, Brian Urlacher tried working in oil pipeline construction. He worked 12 hours a day in 100-degree heat for seven dollars an hour. The experience convinced him of the truth of what his father had told him.

"I've always told my boys to pursue schooling," Troy Lenard said, "to make life easier for themselves than I did. [Working in the oil fields] is no life for anyone."

Yet without the UNM scholarship offer, Urlacher could not see any other future. Many stars of a state championship team would feel discouraged at receiving only two scholarship offers. "But I wasn't too disappointed," Urlacher said. "I felt lucky. Not many kids from Lovington went anywhere. If I didn't get that offer, I'd probably be working in the oil fields now." He added, "I didn't think I was going to need college unless I was going to play football again."

Playing
College Football

The University of New Mexico football team, known as the Lobos, competed in the Western Athletic Conference until 1999, when they joined the new Mountain West Conference. They were not known for their football history.

When Brian Urlacher came to the school in the fall of 1996, the team had won only four conference championships in their entire history (including three in a row from 1962 to 1964). That history was not short; UNM had been one of the first Western schools to play football in 1892 and had been a member of a conference since 1931.

Dennis Franchione, the UNM head coach, had praised Urlacher's abilities in high school. "He always seemed to make plays wherever they put him," Franchione said. "You could always tell he was a very heady and devoted football player."

Urlacher's first two years at UNM, however, were not particularly memorable. Urlacher barely received any playing time as a freshman. Franchione converted Urlacher to linebacker, and although he played in all 11 games, he did not start once and made only eight tackles the entire season. The team finished with a 6–5 record, good for fifth place in the Western Athletic Conference.

The next year was a little better. Urlacher hit the weight room again. By 1997, he weighed 235 pounds (107 kilograms) with an additional 25 pounds (11 kilograms) of muscle. "My dad was tall, so I figured I'd get taller," the 6-foot-4 Urlacher said. "But I never thought I'd be this big." He held the UNM record in the power clean with a lift of 380 pounds (172 kilograms), and he could

UNM AND THE AVIATION BOWL

In the 50 years between 1947 and 1997, the University of New Mexico played in only one bowl game. That was the Aviation Bowl, held on December 9, 1961, in Dayton, Ohio, between UNM and Western Michigan University. It was a cold and miserable day in Dayton, and only 3,500 fans witnessed UNM's 28-12 victory. Many postseason college bowl games have come and gone, but none had as short a life as the Aviation Bowl. Although the game was tentatively scheduled for 1962, the Aviation Bowl was never played again. UNM did not win another bowl game until the 2007 New Mexico Bowl. In 1990, the entire 1961 Aviation Bowl championship team was inducted into the University of New Mexico's Hall of Honor. As of 2011, UNM's record in bowl games was 3–7–1, but the Lobos would forever be the only team to win the Aviation Bowl.

squat lift 570 pounds (259 kilograms). As a sophomore, Urlacher saw more playing time at safety and linebacker and led the team in causing three fumbles. He even won Conference Player of the Week honors against Tulsa University. Still, he had been at college for two years and had yet to start a game.

Urlacher could not really complain, because the UNM team in his sophomore year was the school's best in three decades. The Lobos went 9–4 in 1997 and finished in first place in the newly formed Mountain Division of the Western Athletic Conference. Although Colorado State routed the Lobos in the WAC Championship Game, UNM still received an invitation to the Insight.com Bowl. It was only UNM's second bowl bid since 1947. The Lobos barely lost the game to Arizona, 20-14, in front of almost 50,000 fans in Tucson. Arizona rushed for 209 yards and intercepted four passes to win a hard-fought defensive battle.

BECOMING A STAR

Dennis Franchione had coached UNM for six years with an unimpressive 33–36 record (.478). Franchione, however, cashed in on the success of the 1997 season and left UNM to become the head coach at Texas Christian University. From there, he went on to a successful, financially lucrative, and ultimately controversial coaching career at the University of Alabama and then Texas A&M.

His replacement as UNM head coach was Rocky Long, a quarterback with the Lobos in the 1970s and a former defensive coordinator at UCLA. The hiring of Long turned out to be the best thing for Brian Urlacher. At UCLA, Long had developed an aggressive defensive system made for quick and talented athletes who could make tackles all over the field. Urlacher, now 6-foot-4 and 235 pounds, seemed to have been created for this system. The coach switched his junior linebacker to the freelancing "Lobo" (which means "wolf" in Spanish) position, a cross between a linebacker and a safety, and turned him loose

DON PERKINS, UNM GREAT

Don Perkins was UNM's most famous football alumnus before Brian Urlacher. Perkins was a native of Waterloo, Iowa, where he excelled in track and football and was president of his high school. In 1955, Perkins's team went undefeated and he made the first all-state team as a halfback.

Marv Levy, who later coached the Buffalo Bills to four Super Bowl appearances, was the UNM coach at the time. Levy had coached at Coe College in Iowa in 1953 and 1954, and he persuaded Perkins to play for New Mexico. At UNM, Perkins set 12 records as a three-year halfback starter and led the nation in kickoff returns in 1958. Levy has often said that Perkins was one of the greatest players he ever coached. UNM retired his number (43), the first number retired in school football history.

Perkins's NFL career lasted eight years, all of them with the Dallas Cowboys. He was Rookie of the Year in 1961 and then was named to six Pro Bowls. When Perkins retired just before the 1969 season, only four other NFL running backs had rushed for more than his 6,217 yards. As of 2011, Perkins remains third on the Cowboys' all-time rushing yardage list, trailing only all-time greats Emmitt Smith and Tony Dorsett. He also gained a reputation in the NFL for his fierce blocking and determination on some of the worst teams in Dallas Cowboys history. By 1968, Perkins had helped lead the Cowboys from a hapless expansion team to an NFL power. "I was small," the 5-foot-10, 204-pound (1.78-meter, 92.5-kilogram) Perkins once said, "but I was one that was afraid. When you're scared, you can run real fast."

Perkins played in an era when many fans had a great deal of hostility toward black football players. In the 1960s, Perkins bravely complained about segregation and racism that black players in Dallas experienced, especially when they tried to find housing. The Iowa native was a UNM alumnus who always reflected well on the university.

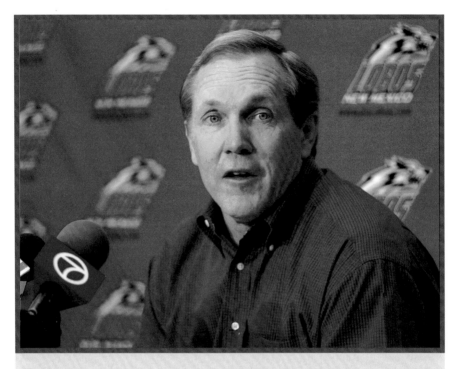

During Urlacher's junior year of college, the University of New Mexico hired Rocky Long to coach the Lobos. Long, an experienced college football coach, developed a unique defensive strategy that took Urlacher off the sidelines and onto the field.

in the center of the defense. Urlacher was free to roam the field, searching for the ball carrier. It was a perfect position for someone of his speed and size.

UNM did not enjoy a successful 1998 season. The Lobos beat Idaho State in their coach's debut but lost 9 of their final 10 games to finish 3–9. Urlacher, however, was one of the team's few bright spots. From a nonstarter as a sophomore, he started every game and was named a first-team all-conference selection. For the season, he made an astounding 178 tackles (still a school record as of 2011) to lead the entire NCAA in tackles. Long's system had turned Urlacher into a national star. "Every game," his coach remembered, "Brian did something that would make you say, 'Wow!'"

One of his classiest plays did not involve football ability. UNM was trailing the University of Texas-El Paso (UTEP)

22-19 in front of a home crowd of 29,812, the seventh largest in UNM history. With seconds remaining, UNM placekicker Mike Ross missed a short field goal that would have sent the game into overtime. A penalty on UTEP gave him another chance with no time on the clock. Unbelievably, Ross missed again and crumpled to the turf in despair. Urlacher's friend Brandon Ridenour noted, "Everybody was walking off the field to the locker room. Brian was the only one to comfort the guy. He went out there and picked him [Ross] up and walked him to the locker room. To me, that's what Brian's all about." In the locker room, Urlacher told reporters that Ross's failure was only one of many; it was just as much his and the defense's fault for letting UTEP score late in the game to take the lead.

Urlacher had such a great year his junior year that he considered leaving UNM early to enter the NFL Draft. Coach Long persuaded him to come back for his senior year and work on becoming a first- or second-round pick. Urlacher decided that the possible rewards were worth the effort. He hoped the decision would translate into a multimillion-dollar contract the next year. After all, he had been starting in college for only one year.

CONSENSUS ALL-AMERICAN

Urlacher's gamble worked out perfectly. In 1999, many college football preview magazines selected him as a preseason All-American safety. Then he had a season that lived up to the hype. At the end of the year, Urlacher was named a Consensus All-American, which meant he earned top honors from every major organization honoring players. He was also Player of the Year in the Mountain West Conference. As a linebacker and free safety, he led the team in tackles (154), recovered fumbles (3), and fumbles caused (5). Urlacher was one of the three finalists for the Jim Thorpe Award, given to the top defensive back in college football. (Tyrone Carter of the University of Minnesota won the award.)

Urlacher was so athletic that Coach Long tried to figure out how to use him in other game situations as a senior. "He wants to return kickoffs," Long said. "And some of the coaches want him to play tailback. They come up with plays for him

URLACHER'S COLLEGE STATISTICS

Here are Brian Urlacher's career statistics while at the University of New Mexico:

YEAR	GAMES	TACKLES			INTERCEPTIONS		
		UA	AST	TOTAL	SCK	PBU	YDS
1996	11/0	7	1	8	0	0	0
1997	13/0	68	34	102	2	3	2/15
1998	12/12	108	70	178	2	8	0
1999	11/11	90	64	154	1	7	1/1
Career	47/23	273	169	442	5	18	3-16

RECEIVING	RECEPTIONS	YDS	AVG	TDS	LONG
1999	7	61	8.7	6	20

PUNT RECEIVING	NUMBER	YDS	AVG	TDS	LONG
1998	3	38	12.7	0	26
1999	10	158	15.8	0	46
Career	13	196	15.1	0	46

KICKOFF RETURNS	NUMBER	YDS	AVG	TDS	LONG
1998	2	15	7.5	0	9
1999	3	79	26.3	0	30
Career	5	94	18.8	0	30

every week." Long used Urlacher on offense in special situations, and Urlacher responded. He caught only seven passes all year, but six of them were for touchdowns. In his very part-time offensive role, he still ended up tying for the Lobo scoring lead with 42 points. He was also UNM's leading punt returner with 10 returns for 158 yards. Years later, he conceded that his college punt return duties might have helped him with his ball-hawking skills.

In a season-opening loss to UTEP, Urlacher recovered a fumble, forced another, and caught a 20-yard pass for a touchdown. In a victory against San Diego State, Urlacher had 20 tackles—14 unassisted—and returned a fumble 71 yards for a touchdown that provided the margin of victory. Against New Mexico State, he had 11 tackles and two touchdown receptions. Urlacher's passion, though, remained on defense. "I try not to gloat," he said, "but when you get a good hit, it just feels so good. You hear the crowd go, 'OOH.'"

Once again, UNM had a disappointing season, finishing 4–7. In fact, throughout Urlacher's college career, the Lobos had given up about 40 points a game. However, his own stock had risen to the point where NFL scouts predicted that he would be a first-round selection in the NFL Draft. Despite only starting for two years, his 442 tackles were third in UNM history. He also added 3 interceptions, 11 sacks, and 11 forced fumbles. He even finished twelfth in the 1999 Heisman Trophy voting for the best college player of the year. Dennis Franchione, who had originally recruited Urlacher, said that he had always expected Urlacher to be a fine player for UNM, but "we never would have predicted the position he's in now."

Meanwhile, Urlacher had become a New Mexico celebrity. Urlacher replica jerseys from high school and college were best sellers. "We've sold tons of 'em," C.C. Massey, a store clerk in Hobbs, New Mexico, said. "People around here are going crazy, he's so popular. Around here, everybody talks about him all the time." Urlacher was recognized everywhere he went in New Mexico.

Urlacher's talent allowed his college coaches to use him in both offensive and defensive plays, and in a variety of field positions. His statistics were impressive, and many predicted he would be selected in the first round of the 2000 NFL Draft.

Urlacher felt a little uneasy with all the publicity. "Most guys would love the position I'm in right now, but I just don't feel comfortable in this position," Urlacher said. "If I was a team- mate of mine, I'd get tired of seeing me talking to the media all the time." Nonetheless, he was looking forward to the NFL Draft with great anticipation. Years later, when he was the NFL Defensive Player of the Year, he was asked if he could have ever imagined such a future when he was a freshman at New Mexico. "No," he said. "I was just happy to make it to college, and then when I got there, I played pretty well and got bigger."

Defensive Rookie of the Year

Brian Urlacher hoped he would be a Top 10 pick in the NFL Draft. Since most pro scouts thought he would play outside linebacker and not free safety in the NFL, Urlacher felt that he had to return to the weight room to bulk up even more. At the NFL "combines" used to evaluate players before the draft, he weighed almost 260 pounds (118 kilograms), ran a 40-yard dash in 4.59 seconds (linebackers average about 4.8 seconds), and bench-pressed 225 pounds (102 kilograms) 27 times. He also put in a fine performance at the 2000 Senior Bowl in Mobile, Alabama. He made five tackles, including one for a loss, and was named the game's defensive Most Valuable Player.

The best linebacker in the 2000 draft was supposed to be LaVar Arrington of Penn State. Arrington was coming out of school as a junior after winning the Dick Butkus Award as the best college linebacker in the United States. After Arrington, no one was quite sure what would happen with the linebackers in the draft. Urlacher was just one possible choice among many: Julian Peterson (Michigan State), Rob Morris (Brigham Young), Keith Bulluck (Syracuse), Ian Gold (Michigan), Raynoch Thompson (Tennessee), and Mark Simoneau (Kansas State).

The Urlacher family held a draft party at a house along the golf course at the Tanoan Country Club in Albuquerque, New Mexico. The house belonged to the parents of Laurie Faulhaber, Urlacher's girlfriend. About 70 friends and family members crowded around the television to see where Urlacher would be playing professional football. Lavoyda Urlacher wanted the Chicago Bears to choose her son. She had been living in Cleveland, a six-hour drive from Chicago, for a little less than a year with Brian's sister, Sheri.

In the NFL Draft, the Bears would be selecting ninth. They expressed interest in Urlacher but also wanted Virginia running back Thomas Jones or Michigan State wide receiver Plaxico Burress if they were available. However, Jones went to the Arizona Cardinals as the seventh pick, and Burress went to the Pittsburgh Steelers as number eight.

Then, Urlacher received a phone call from a Bears executive, minutes before the team's deadline to pick, confirming that Chicago would select him as the ninth pick.

Lavoyda was thrilled. "I'm just so happy for him," she said, "and I'm so glad he's going to Chicago. . . . It's going to be great to go and watch him play every game like I've been doing from sixth grade on." Urlacher admitted that the idea of playing in Chicago near his mother was "an added bonus. It's always great to be closer to your family." Then, within an hour of being drafted by the Bears, he left to board a plane for Chicago.

"We drafted this guy because we think he's got all kinds of upside and potential," Bears head coach Dick Jauron said. "I think we're going to put him in there and let him go." Urlacher

2000 NFL DRAFT

Here are the first-round selections made in the 2000 NFL Draft (an asterisk indicates the player was named to at least one Pro Bowl team; through trades, teams can have more than one pick in the first round):

PICK	NFL TEAM	NAME	POSITION	COLLEGE
1	Cleveland Browns	Courtney Brown	Defensive end	Penn State
2	Washington Redskins	LaVar Arrington*	Linebacker	Penn State
3	Washington Redskins	Chris Samuels*	Offensive tackle	Alabama
4	Cincinnati Bengals	Peter Warrick	Wide receiver	Florida State
5	Baltimore Ravens	Jamal Lewis*	Running back	Tennessee
6	Philadelphia Eagles	Corey Simon*	Defensive tackle	Florida State
7	Arizona Cardinals	Thomas Jones*	Running back	Virginia
8	Pittsburgh Steelers	Plaxico Burress	Wide receiver	Michigan State
9	Chicago Bears	Brian Urlacher*	Linebacker	New Mexico
10	Baltimore Ravens	Travis Taylor	Wide receiver	Florida
11	New York Giants	Ron Dayne	Running back	Wisconsin
12	New York Jets	Shaun Ellis*	Defensive end	Tennessee
13	New York Jets	John Abraham*	Defensive end	South Carolina
14	Green Bay Packers	Bubba Franks*	Tight end	Miami (Florida)
15	Denver Broncos	Deltha O'Neal*	Defensive back	California
16	San Francisco 49ers	Julian Peterson*	Linebacker	Michigan State
17	Oakland Raiders	Sebastian Janikowski	Placekicker	Florida State
18	New York Jets	Chad Pennington	Quarterback	Marshall
19	Seattle Seahawks	Shaun Alexander*	Running back	Alabama
20	Detroit Lions	Stockar McDougle	Offensive tackle	Oklahoma
21	Kansas City Chiefs	Sylvester Morris	Wide receiver	Jackson State
22	Seattle Seahawks	Chris McIntosh	Offensive tackle	Wisconsin
23	Carolina Panthers	Rashard Anderson	Defensive back	Jackson State
24	San Francisco 49ers	Ahmed Plummer	Defensive back	Ohio State
25	Minnesota Vikings	Chris Hovan	Defensive tackle	Boston College
26	Buffalo Bills	Erik Flowers	Defensive end	Arizona State
27	New York Jets	Anthony Becht	Tight end	West Virginia
28	Indianapolis Colts	Rob Morris	Linebacker	Brigham Young
29	Jacksonville Jaguars	R. Jay Soward	Wide receiver	USC
30	Tennessee Titans	Keith Bulluck*	Linebacker	Syracuse
31	St. Louis Rams	Trung Canidate	Running back	Arizona

was the first player taken from the University of New Mexico in the first round of the NFL Draft since the Pittsburgh Steelers chose linebacker Robin Cole in 1977. It was a good omen; Cole turned out to be one of the best linebackers of his generation.

GETTING SETTLED

Urlacher still had some unfinished business before he moved to the Chicago area. In March 2000, not yet 22 years old, he married Laurie Faulhaber. She gushed, "He's the most modest person I know. And he's the most trustworthy person I've ever met. . . . I feel like the luckiest girl in the world." Urlacher also made sure to graduate at UNM with a degree in criminology.

The couple moved to a house in Lake Bluff, Illinois, just north of Chicago. The key feature of the house was a game room complete with air hockey, pool, darts, shuffleboard, video games, and, of course, a Ping-Pong table. "Growing up and seeing how athletes would have these great game rooms, that was a goal of mine," Urlacher said.

Laurie was already pregnant when they moved to Chicago, and their daughter, Pamela, was born on December 13, 2000. Laurie was still thrilled with her spouse in the flush of the first year of marriage. "He's thoughtful, considerate, calls when he's supposed to, is an amazing father, and spoils me rotten," she said. "And he doesn't have a temper. Even when I try to start a fight, he won't."

There was more company for the newlyweds in the house when Brian invited his younger brother, Casey, to live with him. Casey had spent his first two years of college at the New Mexico Military Institute. Now in Illinois, Casey transferred to Lake Forest College with Brian paying the tuition. "I want to be closer to him," Casey said. "I'd like to watch him play, and he'd like to watch me. I really couldn't ask for more in a brother."

Over the next three years, Casey would break many school records while leading Lake Forest to three excellent seasons.

Before Urlacher moved to Chicago to join the Bears, he settled down and married Laurie Faulhaber (*left*). Soon, Laurie gave birth to their daughter, Pamela.

"We respect each other," Brian said. "I look after Casey around the house, try to get him to focus on schoolwork and football—rather than the other things."

Urlacher's contract negotiations with the Bears also went smoothly. He ended up signing a five-year contract worth $8 million. "I'm pretty excited," Urlacher said. "I got signed a lot sooner than people thought. . . . I'm glad because I wanted to be in camp."

"Ever since junior high," his mother said, "Brian always used to tell me when I gave him money, 'I'll pay you back triple when I go pro, mom.' But the payback isn't the money at all. The payback is seeing him make it this far. . . . I'm just proud to see him go after his dream and make it."

It was a strange situation for Urlacher. He was only 22 but married, a father-to-be, and wealthy. It took some getting used to. With his money, Urlacher bought cars for his entire family and an expensive truck for his stepfather. It was a small way of paying Troy Lenard back for raising him. "Brian's always had a real closeness with him," his mother said, "and Brian considers him his real dad." Later that year, Urlacher bought his stepfather a three-bedroom house on 112 acres complete with two fishing ponds in Rising Star, Texas. "He retired me," Troy Lenard said. "He wanted me to come see a game, and I couldn't get off work so he told me to quit. Two days later, I was sitting in the rain in Soldier Field."

Nor did Urlacher forget Lovington High School. When the Wildcats played in their first state championship since 1995, the coach read the team an e-mail that Urlacher had sent. "For you seniors this is possibly your last football game of your career," Urlacher wrote. "Don't leave anything on the field. Don't look back and say, 'I could have done this or I could have done that.' Take advantage of the opportunity you have earned through hard work and discipline." Lovington won the New Mexico championship with a 42-7 victory.

THE CHICAGO BEARS

The team that Brian Urlacher joined was one of the oldest and most famous professional football teams in the United States. The Bears were founded in Decatur, Illinois, in 1919 and moved to Chicago in 1921. The Bears and the Arizona Cardinals (also originally from Chicago) are the only two franchises that have a continuous existence since the NFL's founding.

The Chicago Bears have a proud history that includes nine NFL championships. From 1940 to 1947, they won the title four times. The Bears have the most players in the Pro Football Hall of Fame and have won more games than any other NFL team. (The Bears won their seven hundredth game on December 7, 2008.) For many years, the team was almost synonymous with George Halas, who owned the Bears for an astonishing 63 years and coached the team for 40.

In modern football, Chicago's best seasons were in the late 1980s. The Bears dominated the NFL in 1985 with their revolutionary "46 defense" and lost only one game in the entire season. They won their ninth NFL championship in Super Bowl XX, defeating the New England Patriots 46-10. In that game, the Bears set seven Super Bowl records, including most points and largest margin of victory. The next day, an estimated 500,000 people assembled for a ticker-tape parade in down-town Chicago to greet the team.

Quarterback Jim McMahon and running back Walter Payton led that great Bears team. Chicago's strength, however, was its defense; linemen Richard Dent and Dan Hampton and linebacker Mike Singletary all made the Pro Football Hall of Fame. The Bears' defense allowed the fewest points (198), fewest total yards (4,135), and fewest yards rushing (1,319) of any team during the regular season. They also led the league with 34 interceptions.

After the 1985 championship season, the Bears remained a superb team but failed to return to the Super Bowl. In 1986, the team went 14–2, and the defense allowed an NFL record-low 187 points. In 1987, the Bears won their fourth consecutive division title with an 11–4 mark. The next year, the Bears posted a 12–4 record, tied for best in the NFL. The Bears finished the five-year period (1984–1988) with 62 wins, the most by any NFL team ever in such a span. Yet they were an incredibly frustrating team. For one reason or another, weaker teams often eliminated the Bears from the play-offs.

DIFFICULT EARLY DAYS IN CHICAGO

By 2000, the Super Bowl XX victory and the glory days of the late 1980s were only a nostalgic memory for most Bears fans. The team was mediocre in the 1990s; from 1993 to 1998, Dave Wannstedt coached them to a 41–57 record. He was replaced as head coach by Dick Jauron, a former defensive back and defensive specialist. As Jacksonville's defensive coordinator from 1995 to 1998, Jauron had helped the expansion team reach the play-offs three times. In 1999, Jauron's first season as a head coach, the Bears finished 6–10 and in last place in the National Football Conference (NFC) Central Division. The offense scored only 272 points (25th of 31 teams in the NFL) while the defense allowed 341 points (20th of 31).

LONGTIME RIVALS

The Bears have a fierce rivalry with the Green Bay Packers, a team located 186 miles (299 kilometers) to the north in Wisconsin. The two teams first played each other on November 27, 1921, and have played each other more than 180 times since then. As of 2011, the Bears had a slight edge with 92 wins, 84 losses, and 6 ties. The teams now play each other twice every year, home and away. The games often take place in snow, ice, and subzero temperatures since neither team has a domed stadium. As of 2011, the two teams have won a combined 22 NFL championships including 5 Super Bowls, and have 48 members in the Pro Football Hall of Fame.

This was the team that Urlacher was joining—one with a proud history that had recently fallen on hard times. This situation meant that there was pressure on Urlacher, as the ninth pick in the draft, to perform. One analyst, Skip Bayless, wrote, "Urlacher is the next evolution: a big, tough middle linebacker who'll be able to outrun some backs and receivers." However, John Mullin of the *Chicago Tribune* offered a word of caution: "Urlacher was not the Bears' first choice with the No. 9 pick. . . . If Urlacher is not an immediate impact player, the draft becomes a major disappointment because there were chances to trade up that the Bears passed on because of belief in Urlacher."

Chicago's coaches originally put Urlacher at strongside (known as the "Sam") linebacker. They believed that he would pick up that position more quickly than middle linebacker and be able to contribute to the team immediately. Although Urlacher was used to playing a variety of positions, he struggled at training camp and during exhibition games. Urlacher himself admitted, "I was the worst Sam linebacker ever. I had trouble covering tight ends, I struggled against the run, and I had no technique." He made mental mistakes and was caught out of position. "For the most part, I'm lost," he said. "I'm still looking at one thing instead of the whole picture. I just roamed in college. Here everything is much faster, especially being closer to the line of scrimmage. You don't have as much time to react because the linemen are on you so quick."

Even with his problems, other players recognized his potential. "I was thinking during his rookie training camp, 'He's doing everything wrong, but he's doing it fast,'" the Bears' outside linebacker Warrick Holdman said. "You'd look up on a play and say, 'Man, how did he get on the other side of the field?' We were like, 'He's going the wrong way, but he's going there fast as hell.'"

Before the official season started, Urlacher found himself on the bench, beaten out by Rosevelt Colvin, a fourth-round pick from the year before. He told the media forthrightly, "It's because I didn't play very well and Rosie was playing better."

MOVE TO THE MIDDLE

Urlacher was disappointed in himself. He admitted, "As a rookie, your self-esteem gets lowered, your confidence goes down." He tried, though, not to let this setback get him depressed. The NFL season is long, the situation changes, and players often get injured. The Bears lost their first two games, giving up 71 points in the process. In the second game, middle linebacker Barry Minter hurt his back. Jauron had few choices. He decided to play Urlacher as middle linebacker against the New York Giants in the third game of the season.

It turned out to be the break that Urlacher needed. Against the Giants, he recorded 13 tackles and one sack and reminded everyone why he was a high draft pick. Although the middle linebacker position is harder to learn than strongside linebacker, it was more like the Lobo Back position he played at UNM. He felt much more at home in the center of the field. After the Giants game, Urlacher was the Bears' starting middle linebacker for the rest of the season and the next 11 years.

"If they had put me at [middle linebacker] at the beginning," Urlacher later said, "I don't think I would have done well because I didn't know the calls. I had never called a defense before and I think I would've been nervous and the guys would've gotten on me and yelled at me because I would be screwing up." Years later, Rosevelt Colvin laughed about the way things turned out. Colvin, who became a superb pass-rushing linebacker, joked, "Before I left [the Bears as a free agent], I always used to say he [Urlacher] would never be who he is if it wasn't for me."

Urlacher received the NFC Defensive Rookie of the Month award for October 2000. That month, he accumulated 43 tackles, 4 sacks, and 1 fumble recovery. "I started out poorly," he

In the 1980s, the Chicago Bears were one of the most successful football franchises of the era, even winning Super Bowl XX. The team, however, declined in the 1990s and drafted Urlacher (*above*) in 2000 in the hopes that he would improve the Bears' standing.

said, "so I'm glad both the fans and my teammates are starting to accept me now. It's important to me."

"Brian's the total package," Greg Blache, the Bears' defensive coordinator, marveled. "He has athleticism, size, speed, great eyes, instincts, and intelligence, and guys like playing around him because he's unselfish. I'm certain he's got a hole, but I haven't found it." The Bears' All-Pro offensive tackle James Otis Williams, an 11-year veteran, admitted that he wondered why the team had drafted a college safety to play pro linebacker when most teams do the reverse. "Then we get in the games, and he's twice as fast as in practice and nobody can block him," Williams said.

Urlacher himself said, "I think I got better and better as the season went on." He led the Bears in tackles in 10 of the team's final 13 games. In the eleventh game against the Tampa Bay Buccaneers, Urlacher made a crucial interception to preserve the Bears' 13-10 victory. "He'll say, 'I made the play because of what you guys did,'" Bears defensive tackle Mike Wells said, "but most of the time he'll do it by himself."

Unfortunately, Chicago's record did not reflect Urlacher's development. The Bears did improve from twenty-ninth to sixteenth in yards given up. They started the season 1–7, however, and rallied only slightly to finish 5–11. "You never see him coming. Then he flies out of nowhere and crumbles some poor fool," Williams said. "The problem is, every five plays he's expected to blow up somebody and get the ball back for us. When he doesn't do that, something's wrong."

HE'S GOING TO BE A GOOD ONE

Urlacher finished the 2000 season leading the Bears in total tackles, sacks, solo tackles, and tackles for losses. For his great season, Urlacher easily won the NFL Defensive Rookie of the Year award, receiving 27.5 of the 50 votes cast. "It's amazing. I'm so happy," Urlacher said. "I was pretty sure I wouldn't get it just because we didn't have a very good record. . . . I guess I played well enough." He could take some pride in the fact that neither Bears' middle linebacking greats Dick Butkus or Mike Singletary earned Rookie of the Year honors. "You only get a chance to win Rookie of the Year once," Urlacher said. "It meant a lot."

He was also selected to play in the Pro Bowl as an alternate. The Pro Bowl is the NFL's all-star game; it is an honor to be chosen to play in it. Urlacher even participated in the Pro Bowl that year when one of the players chosen ahead of him was injured. As usual, Urlacher made the most of the opportunity, recording two tackles for the NFC in the game. He was the Bears' first position player in seven seasons to make the Pro Bowl.

Because the Bears lost seven of their first eight games, the Chicago fans had little to cheer. Urlacher became a crowd favorite with his hard-hitting style. Chicago fans had always appreciated defensive players who radiated passion and fearlessness. People began to compare him to former Chicago middle linebacker greats Bill George, Dick Butkus, and Mike Singletary. "From my point of view, he's advancing faster than I anticipated he would," Dick Jauron said. "He's very gifted and a very hard worker, and he loves to play. That's the great thing that shows up on the field, and it is contagious."

"People are going crazy for this kid," said Bob Williams, the president of Burns Sports, a company that matched athletes to advertisers. "He's got the best of Butkus—quick and hard-hitting—and the best of Mike Singletary—respectful of his teammates, the fans, and the other team." Comments like these were a dream come true for Urlacher. With every game, he was playing better, gathering more praise, and increasing his earning potential. "I'm having a great time out there," Urlacher said. "I mean, how great a life is this? To get to knock guys' heads off for 60 minutes and not get thrown in jail?"

"He's playing on emotions right now, a love for the game," said Bears defensive end Bryan Robinson. "And he has great instincts. Just imagine once he gets the true technique and the true factors of playing football, he's going to be a good one."

The Miracle
Season

In Dick Jauron's first two seasons, the Bears had finished last in the NFC Central Division with 6–10 and 5–11 records. No one had any reason to believe that the 2001 season would be particularly different. Most experts picked the Bears to finish last again.

The early signs seemed to confirm these predictions of doom. The team lost their opening game against the defending champion Baltimore Ravens, 17-6. In the next game, the Bears trailed the Vikings 10-0 at halftime and lost their starting quarterback, Shane Matthews, to a hip injury. It looked like another long and frustrating season. In the locker room, players and coaches screamed at one another about the team's poor play. Chicago came out fired up in the second half and somehow upset the Vikings 17-10.

The season quickly turned around; in the next three weeks, the Bears won three games by a combined score of 75-16. In the first five games of the season, the Urlacher-led defense allowed only a miserly 43 points.

The showcase for the defense came in Week 3 against the Atlanta Falcons. Television analysts hyped the game as a showdown between two of the NFL's hottest young stars: Brian Urlacher and Michael Vick. The Bears crushed the Falcons 31-3, and Urlacher was named NFC Defensive Player of the Week for his performance. He dominated the game, registering five tackles, one interception, a sack, and a forced fumble. For good measure, he recovered a fumble at the Bears' 10-yard line and returned it 90 yards for his first career touchdown.

It was coming much easier for him in his second year. "I'm just reacting now," Urlacher said. "I know where I'm going. It just makes so much more sense to me. It's so much more fun." He also became much more adept at dealing with the media pressure, which he admitted "overwhelmed" him his first year.

As middle linebacker, Urlacher called the signals for the defense. That was difficult for him as a rookie just trying to adjust to his first season in professional football. "It's great this year," he said, "because once I hear something it's just a snap in my head and I know what to do. Last year it was like, 'Uhhh, OK, what does this mean again?' Then I'd process it. Now it's just second nature. One thought."

THE AMAZING OVERTIME GAMES

Then came the two games that will live on in the memories of most Bears fans forever. In Game 6, the Bears trailed the San Francisco 49ers 28-9 in the third quarter and lost starting quarterback Jim Miller to an injury. Shane Matthews replaced him and led two long touchdown drives that brought the Bears within two points, 31-29, with less than a minute remaining in the game. When a Chicago running back barreled in for the tying two-point conversion, the game went into overtime and the crowd at Soldier Field went wild.

The high-powered San Francisco offense received the ball first in overtime. On the 49ers' first play, the quarterback threw the ball to All-Pro wide receiver Terrell Owens. Owens seemed to cower from an anticipated brutal hit by Urlacher and gave up on the ball. Mike Brown intercepted the pass and romped 33 yards for the winning score in what was one of the shortest overtime games in NFL history. Chicago fans went crazy.

The following week's result was even more incredible. Chicago trailed the Cleveland Browns 21-7 with less than one minute left in the game. Shane Matthews threw a touchdown pass to close the gap to 21-14 with 28 seconds left. Then Chicago recovered the onside kick. Several short passes moved the ball to the Cleveland 34, but there was only time for one final play. Matthews threw a desperation pass into the end zone that was somehow caught by running back James Allen. The game went into overtime.

The Browns got the ball first, but it did not help them any more than it did San Francisco the previous week. A Cleveland pass was batted up in the air, and safety Mike Brown once again intercepted it and returned it 16 yards for a touchdown. "I don't know what you'd call it—a higher power, destiny. Yeah, destiny, that's the word," Brown said. The 2001 Bears had somehow pulled out their most unlikely victories in a decade. They were 6–1 for the first time since 1991.

THE RENAISSANCE OF THE MIDDLE LINEBACKER

The Chicago Bears virtually invented the middle linebacker position. When the NFL passing game first developed in the 1940s and 1950s, offenses would try to take advantage of the middle area of the field. This zone was often left open by the standard 5-2 defense (five linemen and two linebackers) that most teams played.

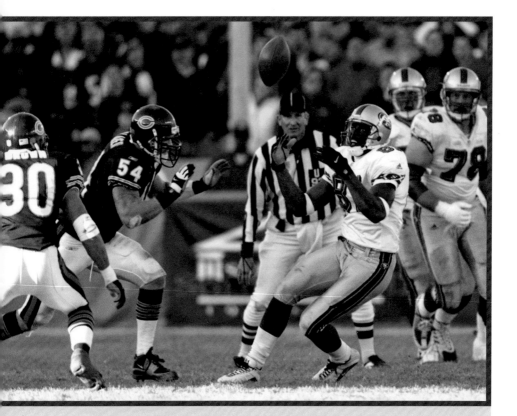

In a game against the San Francisco 49ers, Urlacher (54) charged at wide receiver Terrell Owens (81), causing Owens to fumble the ball. Mike Brown (30) intercepted the pass and scored a touchdown for the Bears.

This changed in 1954 when Bill George, a Bears "middle guard," stood straight up, dropped back three to five yards behind the line of scrimmage, and established a brand-new position. The new defense was called a 4-3-4 or sometimes just a 4-3 (four lineman and three linebackers). Most teams quickly switched over to the new formation. The 4-3 alignment offered defenses more mobility from sideline to sideline. Sometimes the linebackers would "blitz" (charge into the backfield) instead of waiting for the play to develop. The blitz, or "red dog," became one of the signature plays of the NFL.

Sam Huff was the middle linebacker for the New York Giants and the leader of their defense. In 1959, he became the first NFL player to appear on the cover of *Time* magazine. The next year, a famous television special narrated by Walter Cronkite, *The Violent World of Sam Huff*, glamorized the New York Giant and the middle linebacker position. Huff became one of the NFL's first purely defensive stars.

Violent defense became exciting. The heroes of the 1960s and 1970s were rarely glamorous quarterbacks and graceful receivers but crushing middle linebackers like Huff, Joe Schmidt, Ray Nitschke, Dick Butkus, Jack Lambert, and Willie Lanier. The majority of linebackers in the Pro Football Hall of Fame are middle linebackers, including all six named above.

However, the middle linebacker position went into decline in the 1980s and 1990s. In those years, the NFL made rule changes to favor the passing game, and many defenses switched to a 3-4 (three lineman and four linebackers) formation. Outside linebackers like Lawrence Taylor became pass rushing specialists. The no-huddle offense often forced middle linebackers into coverage mismatches, trying to defend against faster wide receivers or bigger tight ends. Coaches began to use the middle linebacker as a part-time defender against the run.

A middle linebacker renaissance began in the late 1990s. Defensive coaches countered the offensive changes by finding quicker players who could cover more ground and stay on the field in all situations. Ray Lewis of the Baltimore Ravens was the best example of this new type of middle linebacker. Lewis won NFL Defensive Player of the Year in 2000 and 2003 and was the MVP of Super Bowl XXXV. As of 2011, most NFL teams have gone back to playing a base 4-3 defense, often with massive defensive tackles to protect the middle linebacker from increasingly large offensive linemen. For example, the Bears shielded Urlacher in 2001 with a pair of huge defensive tackles—330-pound (150-kilogram) Ted Washington and

320-pound (145-kilogram) Keith Traylor—who allowed him to roam across the field.

Urlacher turned professional at the perfect time, right during the rebirth of middle linebacking. Matt Millen, a former inside linebacker, said that Urlacher had "great vision and an uncanny feel for coverage. . . . He's a [college] safety who happened to grow into a linebacker's body, and the possibilities are staggering." Urlacher's trademark was an explosive finishing burst that astonished even experienced football analysts. "Speed sets him above the bar," football executive Mark Dominik said. "Quarterbacks have no idea how fast this guy can close," Greg Blache, the Bears' defensive coordinator, said. "They think, 'I'm fine, I got time. I'll just set and ...' Wham!" Dale Lindsey, Urlacher's linebacker coach, said, "Brian is so quick he can screw up and still go make a play that the normal guy couldn't make if he hadn't screwed up. It's called acceleration and burst."

MIDDLE LINEBACKER—THE BEARS' TRADITION

As the Bears' middle linebacker, Urlacher had to follow a Hall of Fame legacy that reached back three generations: position pioneer Bill George (1952–1966), pulverizing Dick Butkus (1965–1973), and super-intense Mike Singletary (1981–1992). The position in Chicago came with tremendous pressure and expectations but also with a great deal of hype. "Everybody wants to compare me with Butkus and Singletary," said Urlacher in his second year. "I hate it because I haven't done anything yet, and it's not fair to them." However, Urlacher also admitted, "That's the best part of being a linebacker in Chicago. . . . It's a dream come true. Hopefully I can carry on the tradition."

Bill George was the first true middle linebacker in football. He led the Chicago defense in the Bears' 14-10 NFL championship win over the New York Giants in 1963. George was named All-NFL for seven consecutive seasons (1955–1961) and then an eighth in 1963.

George was replaced by Dick Butkus, a Chicago boy who attended the University of Illinois. Butkus was famous for delivering crushing hits on ball carriers. At 6-foot-3 (191 centimeters), 245 pounds (111 kilograms), he was big for his era, and his mere presence in the game intimidated opposing offenses. In 1970, Butkus appeared on the cover of *Sports Illustrated* with the caption, "The Most Feared Man in the Game." Although he never appeared in a play-off game, Butkus is still widely considered the best middle linebacker of all time.

In the 1980s, Mike Singletary was famous for his vicious hits and versatility. Opposing offenses never knew what Singletary was going to do in the 46 defense. Sometimes he dropped into deep coverage; other times he attacked on a blitz. Singletary's celebrated nasty glare became a Bear trademark; it seemed as if his eyes were going to pop right out of his face mask. In 1985, he led a Bears defense that allowed fewer than 11 points per game, as the team posted an impressive 15–1 record. He won the NFL Defensive Player of the Year in 1985 and 1988 and was known as the "Heart of the Defense" when Chicago won Super Bowl XX.

It was only natural that the Chicago media would ask Butkus what he thought about Urlacher. Butkus was complimentary, but he also complained that Urlacher was not mean enough. "He doesn't punish the runner," Butkus said. "With that speed, he can really hurt somebody. . . . Just grabbing people and falling down is not going to get it. . . . If he can develop the punishment factor, some of these running backs have a tendency to chicken out when the going gets tough."

When asked about Butkus, Urlacher said, "From the highlights I've seen, Butkus was a violent dude in a violent era. You could clothesline then, you could head-slap then. He was mean; he could do anything he wanted to back then. We get penalized now if we graze the quarterback's helmet.

"Butkus always has something to say about me, and it's not always good," Urlacher said. "But he's the best middle linebacker ever, and I'm not going to say anything back at him."

Butkus, however, admitted, "I like watching him, I liked watching Singletary, and I'm glad they both played for the Bears. It's really odd how lucky we've been with linebackers. Maybe that's why we haven't been lucky with quarterbacks."

MAKING THE PLAY-OFFS

The Bears lost both games to the Packers in the 2001 season but finished the year 13–3, good enough to win the NFC Central Division for the first time since 1990. Chicago finished an amazing 8–0 in games decided by seven points or less and made the play-offs for the first time since 1994. Coach Dick Jauron had led the greatest turnaround in Bears history and received the 2001 AP Coach of the Year award.

"This team has a lot to be proud of," Jauron said. Jim Miller had the best season of his career at quarterback, starting 13 games and passing for 2,299 yards. Running back Anthony Thomas rushed for 1,183 yards and seven touchdowns and was named Offensive Rookie of the Year. Marty Booker caught a team-record 100 passes for 1,071 yards and eight touchdowns.

Despite the improved offense, the Bears' defense led the way to the play-offs. In 2001, the Bears allowed only 203 points in 16 games, the least in the NFL. With Washington and Traylor clogging up the middle, Chicago finished second in the NFL against the run, forcing quarterbacks to throw more often than they would have liked. As a result, the Bears racked up 48 sacks. Outside linebacker Rosevelt Colvin, the man who originally took Urlacher's position, became a force as a pass rusher with 10.5 sacks. Mike Brown led the team with five interceptions, including the two returned for touchdowns in the back-to-back overtime games. After not sending a single position player to the Pro Bowl from 1994 to 1999, the 2001 Bears sent five players.

The season, however, belonged to Brian Urlacher. He started all 16 games at middle linebacker and led the Bears with 116 tackles. He also ranked among team leaders with six sacks

Using an intense defensive line, the Chicago Bears won the NFC Central Division Championship in 2001. It was an incredibly successful season for the team and for Urlacher, who was named *Football Digest*'s NFL Defensive Player of the Year.

and three interceptions. Urlacher was particularly effective down the stretch. Four times in December, he led the Bears in tackles. He finished fifth in NFL MVP voting, the highest of any defensive player. For his stellar season, Urlacher was a unanimous first-team All-Pro and honored as the NFL Defensive Player of the Year by *Football Digest*.

Urlacher even had some offensive highlights. In the fourteenth game, the Bears were trailing the Washington Redskins 13-10 in the fourth quarter. The Bears lined up for a short field goal that would have tied the game. Instead, Chicago faked the field goal. Brad Maynard, the holder, threw a pass to Urlacher, who went 27 yards untouched into the end zone. The pass

RELAXATION AND PRESSURE

Professional football players perform only once a week, so preparation for the game is important. Urlacher's Sunday morning ritual is probably a little different from that of most other defensive stars. "Every Sunday when I wake up, there is a saltwater fishing show . . . that I watch at 8, and then at 9 o'clock there's another one, and I watch that one until I have to go to the stadium," he told the media. "Then I go over to the stadium, eat a couple of [chocolate chip] cookies, relax a little bit, and listen to my headphones. There's something relaxing to me about watching fishing shows."

After the game is a different story. "Win or lose, I'm up all night," Urlacher said. "I've been that way since college—I'm going over everything in my head: woulda, coulda, shoulda. If I do manage to drift off to sleep, I flip over and wake up and start the process all over again."

helped the Bears beat Washington 20-15, and Urlacher was named NFC Special Teams Player of the Week. "It was fun to have the ball thrown my way," Urlacher said. "If they need me, I will [play a little offense]. . . . But I'm not going to push it."

PLAY-OFFS

On January 19, 2002, the Bears met the Philadelphia Eagles in the divisional round of the NFC play-offs. Philadelphia came to Chicago as the lowest-seeded division winner, and the Bears were heavily favored. Only it did not work out the way that the home crowd hoped. The game was close until the final seconds of the first half, when quarterback Jim Miller left with a separated shoulder. Still, the Bears trailed only 13-7, even though the Eagles finished the half with 230 yards and had the ball for more than 20 minutes, while holding the Bears' offense to 88 yards.

An interception return for a touchdown briefly put the Bears in the lead early in the second half, but then the offense collapsed. Shane Matthews, who replaced Miller, threw for only 66 yards and two interceptions in the half. Chicago's NFL-leading defense did not perform any better. Urlacher led the Bears in tackles, but he had plenty of chances. Eagles quarterback Donovan McNabb racked up 262 yards passing (including two touchdowns) and ran for another touchdown. After earning their first division title in 11 years, Chicago lost their first play-off game to the Eagles, 33-19.

Despite the disappointment, the Bears and Brian Urlacher had good reason to be proud of their season. They had shocked the experts and won the division. Urlacher had proved to be a rare top-10 draft pick who had actually exceeded expectations. He was only 23 years old and bound to get even better. It seemed as if the team had turned a corner.

The next three years, however, would be filled with nothing but frustration for the Chicago Bears.

Regressing:
2002–2004

The 2001 season had been a miracle year for the Bears. Unfortunately, the following season balanced things out. Jim Miller played poorly, lost his starting quarterback job, and never threw another NFL pass after that year (although he did win a Super Bowl ring as the emergency quarterback for the 2004 New England Patriots). Running back Anthony Thomas never repeated the form that made him the NFL Offensive Rookie of the Year. The 2002 Bears led the league in injuries, and many of the coaching decisions were questionable. Chicago began the season with two straight wins. Then the roof fell in. They won only two of their next fourteen games to finish 4–12.

Brian Urlacher had a good season statistically. He led the Bears in tackles in 14 of the 16 games and ranked second in the entire NFL with 151 tackles (behind Miami's Zach Thomas).

He led all NFC defensive players in Pro Bowl voting. He was not happy, however, and was even a little embarrassed by the season's results. The 2002 Chicago defense was atrocious. After leading the NFL the previous year, the Bears finished 25th (out of 31) in least points allowed.

Just the same, the Bears recognized that Urlacher was the heart of their defense as well as a strong marketing tool for the team. Even though Urlacher's contract still had two years left, the Bears decided before the 2003 season to sign him to a long-term contract that would ensure that he played with the Bears for the rest of his career. Negotiations were not difficult, and Urlacher signed a nine-year, $56.65 million contract that would keep him on the Bears until 2011.

"We're a good football team when we're healthy. How good, I don't know," said coach Dick Jauron before the 2003 season. The answer was, better than 2002 but not play-off caliber. The Bears finished 7–9 in 2003, and Jauron was fired at the end of the season. He had coached the Bears for five seasons (1999–2003), finishing with a 35–45 regular-season record and one play-off appearance. He later went on to coach the Buffalo Bills, but, as of 2011, Jauron had coached 10 seasons in the NFL and had finished only 1 of them with a winning record—the magical Bears season of 2001.

THE LOVIE SMITH ERA BEGINS

After a long search, the Bears hired Lovie Smith as the thirteenth head coach in their history in 2004. When Chicago hired him, Smith became only the seventh African-American coach in the NFL.

Smith grew up in Big Sandy, Texas, a tiny farming town between Dallas and Shreveport, Louisiana. Money was tight in Smith's family, and he lived a small-town existence in a one-stoplight town very similar to Brian Urlacher's childhood in Lovington.

Smith received only one scholarship offer, to the University of Tulsa, where he was a two-time All-American linebacker. After a short attempt at playing professional football, he returned to Big Sandy as an assistant coach. He coached high school for three years. In 1983, Tulsa hired him as a linebackers coach (1983–1986), and then he worked as an assistant at Wisconsin (1987), Arizona State (1988–1991), Kentucky (1992), Tennessee (1993–1994), and Ohio State (1995).

Smith began his NFL coaching career as a linebacker coach for the Tampa Bay Buccaneers under head coach Tony Dungy. At Tampa Bay, he helped develop several Pro Bowl linebackers. After four years with the Buccaneers, the St. Louis Rams hired Smith to the key position of defensive coordinator. While in St. Louis, Smith improved the Rams' defense, which went from giving up a league-worst 29.4 points per game in 2000 to allowing only 17.1 points per game in 2001 (third best in the NFL). The Rams won the 2001 NFC Championship Game and lost to the New England Patriots in Super Bowl XXXVI.

Smith had a reputation for being calm and especially loyal. He rarely yelled at players and tried to avoid criticizing them in the media. "Most of the perception about coaching is you have to scream and yell at the players to get your point across. That isn't the case," Smith said. "Players want you to teach them, to help them with their profession, to get them better. I'd say my style of coaching is positive reinforcement. . . . What has always motivated me is people saying, 'Hey Lovie, you can do it. You have what it takes.'"

Once again, Brian Urlacher would be playing under a defensive specialist. The defensive scheme, though, changed a little. Lovie Smith played more "Cover-2," a defense that gave Urlacher many more pass coverage responsibilities in the middle of the field between the two safeties. Smith's defense also used slimmer, faster linemen instead of defensive tackles who tied up linemen to allow linebackers to make plays. Urlacher would be required to shed more blocks than he had in previous seasons.

The Chicago Bears hired Lovie Smith (*above, with Urlacher*) to lead the team as the new head coach in 2004. Smith, a coach who believed in teaching and encouragement, was a defense specialist and expanded Urlacher's responsibilities on the field.

The Lovie Smith era did not get off to a good start. Three games into the 2004 season, Rex Grossman, the Bears' newest quarterback, damaged his knee ligaments while scrambling for a touchdown and missed the remainder of the season. Smith used three other quarterbacks during the year as the Bears struggled. Chicago's defense improved from twenty-second in the NFL in 2003 to thirteenth in 2004. Unfortunately, the Bears were dead last in eight offensive categories. The team finished

5–11 in Smith's first year of coaching; it was Chicago's eighth losing season in the past nine.

MISSING GAMES

Urlacher had had a solid 2003 season although, for the first time in his career, he did not register a forced fumble or an interception. However, he led the Bears with 116 tackles (87 solo tackles) while holding or tying for the team lead in tackles in nine games. He played in his fourth consecutive Pro Bowl and had yet to miss a game for the Bears—64 games in a row.

The 2004 season would be different. In the first no-contact practice of training camp, Urlacher badly pulled a hamstring and missed the rest of the preseason. He did manage to return for an opening-game loss to the Detroit Lions. The next game was against the hated Green Bay Packers. The Bears were smarting because they had lost to the Packers seven straight times.

In a dramatic game, the Bears led 7-3 with less than two minutes left in the first half. Green Bay was driving down the

BIG SANDY'S AMAZING SEASON

Lovie Smith played defensive end and linebacker on the amazing Big Sandy High School (in Big Sandy, Texas) team of 1975, one of the greatest high school football teams in history. In that year, Big Sandy went 14–0 and won the state title. The team scored 824 points (59 a game) while the defense allowed only 15 points (11 shutouts) all season. Running back David Overstreet, who would later play for the Miami Dolphins, had nearly 3,000 yards rushing and scored 52 touchdowns. He averaged an incredible 23.8 yards a carry.

field and inside the Bears' 20-yard line. A Packer running back took a handoff and looked as though he was going to score. At the 5-yard line, Urlacher applied a nasty hit and knocked the ball loose for a fumble. Safety Mike Brown picked up the ball and, shades of 2001, raced 95 yards for a touchdown, making the score 14-3 at the half. The Bears ended up winning the game 21-10. Urlacher had a team-high 14 tackles in the game and earned NFC Defensive Player of the Week honors for his efforts.

Unfortunately, the victory over the Packers would be the high point of the season for the team and for Urlacher. In the game, they lost Brown for the season with an Achilles tear and cornerback Charles Tillman for most of the season with a knee injury. Urlacher reinjured his hamstring and missed the next two games (both losses). That snapped Urlacher's string of 64 consecutive starts with the Bears. He said:

> I'd never pulled a muscle, so when I hurt it in training camp, I didn't know what to think. They told me four to six weeks; I figured three. The first two [regular-season] games, it felt awesome. Then I reinjured it. It's a bad feeling, man, like it's going to pop anytime. It feels like I'm not going all out. I'm taking short steps; I can't really stride.

By the time Urlacher returned, Chicago's season had collapsed. In the third game, quarterback Rex Grossman was injured, and the team once again had to make do with a series of backup quarterbacks. The results were predictable, with the Bears' offense finishing last in the NFL in passing yardage and in total offense.

Urlacher did earn Player of the Week honors in a Game 7 victory against the San Francisco 49ers when he recorded his third career two-sack game and tied for the team lead with

In a game against the Bears' longtime rivals, the Green Bay Packers, Urlacher sacked running back Ahman Green (*above*), causing Green to fumble and drop the ball. Bears safety Mike Brown seized the ball and ran 95 yards down the field to score a dramatic touchdown.

nine tackles. The team won the next two games to bring their record to 4–5. In a 19-17 victory against Tennessee, however, Urlacher was seriously injured when an opposing player accidentally kicked him in the leg late in the game and popped a bursa sac. He needed major surgery to relieve the swelling in his left knee and calf, and he missed two games. His absence was immediately noticed when the Indianapolis Colts annihilated Chicago's defense, 41-10. Urlacher returned from his leg injury against the Minnesota Vikings in Game 12 but reinjured his hamstring in the next game. The Bears lost their final four games to finish at 5–11.

Urlacher was named an alternate for the Pro Bowl despite missing seven games, but some wondered if he did not just make it on his prior reputation. He did lead all middle linebackers in the NFL with 5.5 sacks. The injuries, though, were a worry. He had just finished his fifth season, and many linebackers did not last longer than that, especially those who played with as much abandon as Urlacher. Chicago's futility also drove him crazy. "It's been . . . terrible, frustrating. I can't get my mind off of it," Urlacher said. "We went 13–3 in 2001 and started 2–0 the next year. Then bam!—it all fell apart. I don't know what happened. We stopped winning close games, and two years later we're still struggling. It's not fun, and the off-season is horribly long."

A MESSY PERSONAL LIFE

Football was not the only frustrating aspect of Brian Urlacher's life. He had moved to Chicago right out of college as a husband and a father-to-be. He had to learn to be a professional football player at the most famous position on the Chicago Bears in a football-obsessed city. His success had made him wealthy and a local celebrity, but that brought its own stress and challenges. It was all a little strange; Urlacher noted, "Everywhere I go, I see people wearing my jersey. It's cool because we have the best fans in football. But it's crazy. It blows me away; that's all I can say about it."

One casualty of Urlacher's newfound stardom was his personal life. The strangeness of his situation was too much for his marriage. He filed for divorce from Laurie in 2003, and the couple divorced the next year after four years of marriage.

The divorce was fairly amicable but complicated by Pamela, their three-year-old daughter. "My wife and I are divorced now," Urlacher explained to the media. "We get along great, but she moved to Phoenix with my daughter. I don't see my daughter as much as I'd like to, but my ex is really good about letting her come to stay with me. She knows I can't be without her for too long." Apparently, Brian and Laurie had not completely separated, because Laurie became pregnant again in 2004.

Then Urlacher's life got even more complicated. In 2004, he had a brief affair with Tyna Robertson, who also became

CASEY URLACHER

It seemed ideal when Casey Urlacher moved in with his big brother in 2000, but that situation did not work out completely as planned. Casey broke a host of records as a linebacker and running back at Lake Forest College and won the conference Defensive Player of the Year award after his senior season in 2002. He graduated with a degree in business, but his main goal was to get into the NFL, maybe even to join Brian on the Chicago Bears. "Playing with Brian would be awesome," Casey said. "We've talked about it. He'd like it a lot, and my family and a lot of people in Chicago would get a big kick out of it."

Brian did his best to boost his brother's chances. "He's a real fun player to watch," he told the press. "Whatever he hits goes backwards. From what I've seen of this league [the NFL], he can play up here." Casey, though, was not chosen in the 2003 NFL Draft. He practiced with the Bears but was cut by Dick Jauron and ended up playing for the Chicago Rush and the Nashville Kats of the Arena Football League.

pregnant. Urlacher was recently divorced and in his twenties in the big city, but Robertson was a particularly reckless choice. Her reputation was not enhanced by her unsuccessful claims of sexual assault against dancer Michael Flatley in 2003. The case was thrown out of court, and Flatley sued Robertson for fraud and extortion. (In 2008, a judge found that Robertson had defamed Flatley and ordered her to pay him $11 million.)

Meanwhile, Urlacher moved back in with his ex-wife, and their second daughter, Riley, arrived on April 1, 2005. Seven weeks later (on May 20), Tyna Robertson gave birth to a son,

At 6-foot-1 (1.85 meters) and 240 pounds (109 kilograms), Casey resembled a smaller version of his more famous brother. "They couldn't be more different personality-wise," Lavoyda Urlacher said, "but Casey always had the same goals Brian did when they were smaller, to play in the NFL. I think the biggest thing in [trying out] is measuring up with his older brother. That can be tough."

"I'm done," Casey said in 2007 about his NFL dreams. "And I'm happy all the hard workouts are behind me. I don't have to constantly push myself to lift weights and try to get to the next level." Instead, he used his business degree to open a chic nightclub, Bon V, in downtown Chicago.

"People always want to know if it upset me living in Brian's shadow, but I've never felt that way," Casey said. "He's a great guy, a great brother, and a great father to his kids. . . . I'm happy for him. That might be hard for a lot of people to believe, but I'm a huge Brian Urlacher fan."

Kennedy. Urlacher immediately hired a lawyer to establish paternity, custody, and support for Kennedy. He hoped to live together again with Laurie and their two daughters. In a September 2005 petition to the court, Urlacher claimed that he should be the "primary residential parent" for Kennedy because he could provide a "stable home environment." He cited his experience with "raising an infant child." While that case was pending, however, Brian and Laurie separated again.

Unfortunately, these very private events played out in newspapers, magazines, and television around the country. Urlacher was a celebrity, and the American public was fascinated by scandal. Media scrutiny of his private life was part of the price he paid for being famous. "I realize in my position that's the way it goes," he said. "Everything you do is put out there, but I'll have to watch what I do, I guess."

He did not make it easier on himself when he was seen in the fall of 2003 in Las Vegas with hotel heiress Paris Hilton. Hilton was a constant presence in the nation's gossip pages and the object of much ridicule. Urlacher tried to put an innocent spin on the situation. "I get to meet a lot of cool people, obviously, with what I do," he said. "It was a coincidence that I got to meet her in Vegas, and we kind of hung out a little bit and that's about it." His private life, however, was becoming a punch line for football talking heads and gossip columnists. On and off the field, the period from 2002 to 2004 was a frustrating one in Urlacher's life.

The Defense Paves the Way

Sports Illustrated's 2005 NFL Preview edition predicted that the Chicago Bears were the worst team in football, ranking them 32nd out of 32 teams. Rex Grossman, the team's starting quarterback, suffered his second major injury in two seasons when he broke his ankle in a preseason game and missed most of the season. It was the Chicago quarterback jinx again; Grossman had been reliably injury-free in high school and college.

In the fourth week, Chicago led the Cleveland Browns in the fourth quarter. Then the defense gave up two late touchdown passes to lose the game. That left the Bears' record at 1–3, and it looked like another long season.

Amazingly, the Bears rallied to achieve one of their best seasons. Head coach Lovie Smith kept telling the players, "Hey fellas, come on, let's circle the wagons. Don't play for me, play for the guy next to you and the guy next to you. Think about what you've been doing this whole off-season, think about what you've been working for. Don't make all that work for nothing. . . . Let's just pull together."

After the slow start, the Bears roared into first place with eight straight victories, and they won 10 of their final 12 games. The team used five different starting quarterbacks during the season and finished twenty-sixth in points scored. Rex Grossman did come back to start Game 15 and helped lead Chicago to a narrow 24-17 victory over the Packers in Green Bay. It was Chicago's first sweep of their rivals since 1991. With the victory, the Bears became the unlikely champions of the NFC North and clinched a play-off spot with one game to spare.

How did they do it? Chicago's success was based around their superb defense, which finished first in the NFL in fewest points allowed and second in least yardage allowed. These totals included a meaningless final game in Minnesota in which the Bears played many substitute players and gave up 34 points. Defensive end Adewale Ogunleye, signed as a free agent from the Miami Dolphins, led the team with 10 sacks. Agile defensive tackle Tommie Harris earned the first of three straight trips to the Pro Bowl, and linebacker Lance Briggs began a string of four consecutive Pro Bowl appearances. Cornerback Nathan Vasher made the Pro Bowl by intercepting eight passes and returning one of them for a touchdown against Green Bay. The brilliant defense set an NFL record for fewest points allowed in eight games at home, and coach Lovie Smith won the AP NFL Coach of the Year.

Brian Urlacher had the biggest year of all, receiving the AP NFL Defensive Player of the Year award. It was the highest honor that a defensive player in the NFL could receive. He polled an overwhelming 34 of the 50 votes from sportswriters and broadcasters on a national panel. Healthy again, he started all 16 regular-season games in 2005 at middle linebacker and tallied 121 tackles to lead Chicago for the fifth time in six years. In the team's run to the play-offs, Urlacher recorded 10 or more solo tackles in six straight games.

AT THE PEAK OF HIS CAREER

With his Defensive Player of the Year award, Urlacher joined a select group that included linebackers Ray Lewis, Mike Single-tary, Lawrence Taylor, Jack Lambert, and Derrick Brooks. At 27 years old, he was now at the peak of his career. He had sufficient experience to recognize almost any situation but not enough years to be worn down by age, multiple injuries, and general pounding. At 6-foot-4 and 250 pounds, he retained the remarkable combination of speed, size, tackling ability, and instinct that made him a menace at middle linebacker. He was equally at home making tackles at the line of scrimmage or dropping back 30 yards downfield to cover speedy running backs and wide receivers.

Detroit Lions quarterback Jon Kitna said that Urlacher was "special because he's got size and speed but also because of his football IQ, which is something that a lot of people are missing when they talk about Brian." Urlacher used every bit of his experience to try to gain an edge in games. "You can usually pick stuff off lineman," he said. "Sometimes they lean, sometimes they sit back in their stance or don't put their hand down, which means they're going to pass. And sometimes it doesn't work at all."

Urlacher often jumped into the gap right in front of the offensive center. There, he could listen to the quarterback and pretend to blitz. Seattle's quarterback, Matt Hasselbeck, said, "He leans in so he's right in your face, and you start to audible and then he starts to audible, except you're not really sure if he's audibling or not. It's pretty intense, although it's more intense at Soldier Field [in Chicago], with the crowd noise."

As he got older, Urlacher had also taken more of a leadership role with the Bears. Because he was a hard worker, he commanded respect from his teammates through his actions during practice and games. Urlacher said:

> I lead by example. But if I get pissed off enough, I say something. It usually isn't rah-rah; it's more complaining. In our game against Tampa, we gave up 10 points early and were playing terrible. At halftime, I gathered the defense and expressed myself: Basically, it was "BLEEP, BLEEP, BLEEP." I usually don't do stuff like that, but when we make stupid mistakes, it makes me mad.

"When he messes up, he owns up to it. When you mess up, he jumps down your throat. That's why he's our leader," said Pro Bowl defensive end and teammate Alex Brown. Another Bears All-Pro linebacker, Lance Briggs, marveled, "He's a competitor in everything he does. . . . He's going to be the first to tell you when you screw up. He'll be the first to tell everybody he screwed up when he screwed up. The anecdote is just him wanting to compete on every play. He wants to win on every play."

"I think I'm getting better every season," Urlacher said. "That's really all I try to do, is just watch film, get better, and make my technique better." Lovie Smith simply said, "I think he is the best player in football."

NOT AGAIN!

The Bears were particularly confident going into the 2005 play-offs. They had beaten the Carolina Panthers, 13-3, in Chicago earlier in the season. "They might think they can beat us, but we know we can beat them," said one Bears defender. Before a loud home crowd of more than 62,000, however, the game quickly went wrong for the Bears. On Carolina's first offensive series, speedy receiver Steve Smith caught a 58-yard touchdown pass before a minute had gone by.

Carolina led 10-0 in the first quarter and was threatening to score again when Urlacher intercepted a pass. The Bears cut the gap to 23-21 early in the fourth quarter, but again the defense could not hold. Panthers quarterback Jake Delhomme completed five passes for 45 yards and then threw a 1-yard touchdown pass. The Bears never led and were once again eliminated from the play-offs without winning a game.

The Bears had depended on Urlacher and their defense throughout the year, but the defense let them down in this game. The Panthers ran up 434 yards of total offense, and Carolina receiver Steve Smith caught 12 passes for 218 yards and two touchdowns. Delhomme threw for 319 yards and three touchdowns.

Since 1990, only three teams with a first-round bye had lost their first play-off game. Unfortunately for Urlacher, two of those losses were by the Bears—in 2001 and 2005. The only other time this happened was when the Carolina Panthers beat the St. Louis Rams and defensive coordinator Lovie Smith at home in 2003.

Yet despite the disappointment of the play-offs, the 2005 Chicago Bears proved to their fans and detractors that they were a team on the rise. Once again, the future looked quite bright.

SUPER SEASON

Over the previous three seasons, Rex Grossman had played in just eight regular-season games at quarterback for the Bears. In 2006, however, he started all 16 games, and Chicago's offense reappeared with him. Chicago won its first seven games, then cruised to victory in six of its final nine for a 13–3 record and their second consecutive NFC North title.

The biggest change was in the Bears' offense. To everyone's amazement, Chicago finished second in the NFL in points scored and fifteenth in total yards. Grossman had an effective

In the 2005 season, Urlacher expanded his role as a veteran Bears player and became one of the team's leaders. His teammates admired his work ethic, honesty, and relentless playing style.

if unbelievably erratic season. He managed to simultaneously have both the best (23 touchdowns and 3,193 passing yards) and the worst (20 interceptions, five fumbles lost) season in the Bears' history. The electrifying Devin Hester recorded six return touchdowns, including a punt return in his NFL debut and a record-tying 108-yard touchdown from a missed field goal.

The defense, however, was once again the bedrock on which Chicago rested. Mark Anderson, only a fifth-round draft pick, led the team with 12 sacks, the most by a Bear since Richard Dent in 1993. That total broke the Bears' rookie record, previously held by Urlacher. Defensive tackle Tommie Harris and linebacker Lance Briggs had huge years and made the Pro Bowl again. Cornerbacks Charles Tillman and Ricky Manning Jr. both had five interceptions and superb seasons.

All the defensive players took enormous pride in their accomplishments. In Week 5, the Bears were leading the Buffalo Bills (coached by Dick Jauron) 40-0 with just minutes left in the game when the Bills scored a garbage touchdown to make it 40-7. Chicago's defenders were extremely upset and declared that they would not allow a breakdown like that again. "The guys right now are upset about [losing] the shutout," Lovie Smith said after the game. "We felt like we should have gotten it. But they did a lot of good things."

Urlacher had an appropriately super season, and several publications named him first-team All-Pro. Despite often dropping back 30 yards in pass coverage, Urlacher led the NFC with 141 tackles, the second-highest total of his career. He started all 16 games for the fifth time in his career and led or tied for team lead in tackles during eight regular-season games. In Game 10, he intercepted a pass against the New York Jets to preserve a victory and a shutout. Teams, however, did not often test him. As Jon Kitna, the Lions' quarterback, said, "With Urlacher out there, throwing down the middle is buyer beware."

Urlacher's greatest game of the year was a Monday night game against the Arizona Cardinals in October. The Bears trailed

20-0 at halftime, and the offense was horrible. Urlacher and the defense, however, saved the game. Mark Anderson caused the Arizona quarterback to fumble, and Mike Brown recovered it and scored a touchdown. Later, Urlacher yanked the ball free from Cardinal running back Edgerrin James, and Charles Tillman returned it 40 yards for another touchdown. Late in the game, Devin Hester broke free on an 83-yard punt return for a touchdown, and the Bears won 24-23 without the offense scoring a touchdown. Pro Bowl center Olin Kreutz was in awe. He said, "Brian Urlacher wasn't going to lose that game. He willed our team to victory in the second half. It's about time people realized how truly great he is." Urlacher made 19 tackles in the game, and the Bears made NFL history by becoming the first team to rally from 20 points down without an offensive touchdown.

ROAD TO THE SUPER BOWL

The Bears' first opponent in the play-offs was the Seattle Seahawks, who were coming off a miracle win over the Dallas Cowboys in the opening round. The Bears had previously crushed the Seahawks, 37-6, in October. The Chicago players had to remind themselves that they had been overconfident the year before against Carolina and paid for it. "Last year we were in this position, and we were unable to finish the season up the way we wanted," Lovie Smith said. "We just talked about all we've gone through this year and that it would be a shame not to finish on a high note."

Brian Urlacher particularly felt the pressure. In his seven seasons, the Bears had played two postseason games. Both times, they lost at home, and the defense surrendered at least 29 points in each defeat. Another home play-off loss would represent the low point of Urlacher's career. "We're definitely more experienced," he said. "We don't want to lose. We've had home field now three times. We need to take advantage of it this time."

He became increasingly sensitive when people criticized the Bears. "People have been on our backs all year long,"

Urlacher said before the play-offs. "They've consistently told us how bad we are. We're the worst 13–3 team of all time." When the media asked him questions, he became unusually sarcastic. Asked about the Bears' past play-off disappointments, he said, "Thanks for bringing that up." Only a victory would make the questions go away.

Chicago held a 21-14 lead at halftime, but the Seahawks put 10 points on the board to start the second half. It looked as if Chicago was about to blow another season, when Robbie Gould's 41-yard field goal into the wind with 4:24 remaining in the fourth quarter tied the game 24-24.

In overtime, Grossman threw a 30-yard completion to Rashied Davis on third down and 10 to give the Bears a first down at the Seattle 36-yard line. A few plays later, Gould kicked a 49-yard field goal with 10:02 left in overtime to give the Bears a thrilling 27-24 win. The victory sent Chicago into the NFC Championship Game for the first time since 1988.

The Bears' defense had been shaky. Chicago had given up more than 300 yards for the seventh straight game after being the only NFL team to hold each of its first 10 opponents under that total. "We know we didn't play our best game today," Urlacher said afterward. "We pride ourselves on being a second-half team, and they really took it to us in the third quarter. But we also did enough to win." Chicago's defense registered three sacks and stopped the Seahawks when it mattered most. "We were 0–2 in this game," Urlacher said. "We're over that hump finally. It feels great. It's exciting for our team. We made the plays when we had to. We got a monkey off our backs."

In the NFC Championship Game, the Bears had to face the New Orleans Saints. The Saints were a difficult team to play. New Orleans had turned around a 3–13 season in 2005 to finish 10–6 in 2006, the most successful season in the team's history. The Saints had a powerful offense headed by a fine quarterback in Drew Brees and two dangerous running backs

As one of the team's best players, Urlacher was constantly scrutinized. He went into the 2006 play-offs season feeling this pressure and helped lead his team to victory against the Seattle Seahawks. Above, Urlacher (54) and Bears safety Chris Harris (46) intercept a Seahawks pass.

in Reggie Bush and Deuce McAllister. Urlacher admitted, "New Orleans will be a tough test because they have a great offense."

The Saints were also sentimental favorites. After Hurricane Katrina almost destroyed New Orleans in August 2005, the Saints were not able to play any home games for the entire 2005 season. There was talk that the Saints, perennial losers in New Orleans, would leave the city permanently. In the fall of 2006, the Saints returned to play all of their regular home games at the Louisiana Superdome. To everyone's astonishment, the team played brilliantly and seemed to reflect the city's refusal to die. As New Orleans rebuilt, the team provided an inspiring part of the recovery story. Almost all neutral and casual fans were rooting for the Saints to defeat the Bears and make it to the Super Bowl for the first time.

In the sleet of frozen Soldier Field in January, however, the Bears had an advantage. New Orleans was a "dome" team, unused to playing in snowy conditions. The Bears converted three early turnovers into three field goals and then scored on a long drive to take a 16-7 halftime lead. The Saints closed the gap to 16-14 on an 88-yard touchdown pass. Then the Bears' defense took over. Drew Brees grounded the ball in his own end zone, which resulted in a safety. Adewale Ogunleye and Nathan Vasher created key turnovers, and Chicago scored the last 23 points to pull away for a convincing 39-14 win and the Bears' first trip to the Super Bowl in 22 years.

Once again, Chicago's defense had given up more than 300 yards. The Saints outgained the Bears in total yards, 375-335, and Brees passed for 354 yards and two touchdowns. The defense, though, had stuffed the Saints' ground game; Bush had only 19 yards rushing, and McAllister 18 yards. Chicago's defense had also caused the four turnovers (three fumbles and one interception) that led to the Bears' victory. Urlacher had four tackles in the game but also a career-high four passes broken up. After the game, defensive end Ogunleye complained that "when you see everyone picking the Saints, the thing is we won 14 games, now 15, by playing sound defense and we have been doing a good job all season. We know they are coming in as a No. 1 offense and we stepped up to the plate."

SUPER BOWL XLI

Every Super Bowl needs hype, and the focus of Super Bowl XLI was Peyton Manning, the NFL's best quarterback, versus

Urlacher and his teammates brought glory back to the Bears franchise when they beat the New Orleans Saints in the 2007 NFC Championship Game. The team's last NFC championship victory was in 1995.

Brian Urlacher, the game's best middle linebacker. Super Bowl XLI marked the fifth time that the game was a showdown between one conference's top defense and the other's top offense. The top defense prevailed in all four previous meetings. Just the same, the Bears were huge underdogs against the Indianapolis Colts.

The Bears' defense had not been playing well in recent games. Before Game 12, the Bears had allowed only two opponents to score more than 20 points. After that, Chicago's opponents scored more than 20 points in five straight games. The encouraging news was that Chicago had broken that streak by holding the Saints to 14 points in the NFC Championship Game. "If we play hard and physical," Urlacher said, "we should have a chance to win the game."

Urlacher found himself the subject of pregame publicity when the NFL fined him an astonishing $100,000 for wearing a cap during the Super Bowl media day that promoted a sponsor not authorized by the league. NFL rules prohibited any gear that advertised any product except by a designated NFL sponsor. Urlacher received his fine for drinking Vitamin Water and wearing a Vitamin Water hat. As it turned out, the company paid the fine by donating the $100,000 to charity.

Super Bowl XLI was the first Super Bowl played in the rain. The moisture made the game extremely sloppy. Players slipped and fell on the soggy field while the ball squirted through their hands. The two teams exchanged fumbles on consecutive plays and set a record for turnovers in the first quarter (four), with six in the first half. Lavoyda Urlacher was there with Pamela, Urlacher's six-year-old daughter. "She just keeps saying, 'Nana, I'm cold,'" Lavoyda Urlacher said. "And I keep saying, 'We have to stay here and watch Daddy play.'"

The game started with a bang. The rain did not hinder Bears return specialist Devin Hester, who ran back the opening kickoff 92 yards for a touchdown to give Chicago the earliest lead in Super Bowl history. Peyton Manning and Rex Grossman then exchanged touchdown passes, and Chicago led 14-6 after the first quarter.

From that point on, the game turned ugly for the Bears. Chicago committed several turnovers and trailed 16-14 at half-time. They were still in the game at the beginning of the fourth quarter, trailing only 22-17, with the ball at their own 20-yard line and 13:38 left in the game. Four plays later, a Colts defensive back intercepted a wobbly Grossman pass and returned it 56 yards for a touchdown to put the game away. Chicago, the team that had led the NFL in takeaways that season, finished the game with five turnovers. "A frustrating loss," Grossman

ABOUT TIME

Super Bowl XLI made history as the first game in which both opposing head coaches were African American. Chicago's Lovie Smith became the first African-American head coach to lead his team to a Super Bowl. He beat Indianapolis's Tony Dungy, his good friend and mentor, by only a few hours.

The NFL's first black coach, Art Shell of the Oakland Raiders, was hired in 1989. By that time, two-thirds of NFL players were African American. As of 2002, the league still had only two black head coaches. That year, threatened by an antidiscrimination lawsuit, the NFL responded with the Rooney Rule, which required NFL teams to interview at least one minority candidate when filling a head coaching position. By the beginning of 2006, the NFL had seven African-American head coaches. In 2011, the league continues to have seven African-American head coaches.

said. "There were definitely opportunities for us to take that game, and we didn't do it."

In a contest billed as a showdown between Manning and Urlacher, the Colts won 29-17. Both stars played well but not exceptionally. Manning completed 25 of 38 passes for 239 yards with one touchdown and one interception. In the absence of another candidate, he won the Super Bowl MVP award.

Urlacher made seven solo tackles and assisted on three others. The defense had given up only 22 points to the best offensive team in the NFL (the Indianapolis defense scored the team's last touchdown). However, the NFC leading defense had given up an amazing 430 yards, and the Colts' ball-control offense had worn down the Chicago defense.

Urlacher was incredibly disappointed, but he impressed people after the game with his willingness to take responsibility for the loss and not blame other people. "You have to play better if you expect to win the Super Bowl. That's all there is to it," he said. "We couldn't make plays on both sides of the ball when we needed to. There's a lot of things we could've done—tackle better, cover better, pursue better. It's not just one guy. It's all of us, but it starts with me."

The End
Draws Near

The trip to the Super Bowl after the 2006 season had raised the expectations of the Bears and their fans. Now, they expected to return to the big game as soon as possible. Under those circumstances, the following two seasons were extremely disappointing.

In 2007, the Bears finished 7–9 and in last place in the NFC North after dominating the division the previous two seasons. Many defensive players suffered serious injuries, and the offensive line crumbled. Quarterback Rex Grossman played so poorly that, by the fourth game, coach Lovie Smith replaced him with Brian Griese. Not many NFL teams start three quarterbacks in a season. Yet in 2007, the Bears did it for an amazing fifth time in seven years.

The defense, so outstanding in 2006, was part of the problem. For a variety of reasons, the Bears' defensive ranking fell from fifth overall in 2006 to twenty-eighth in 2007. In the fourth game against Detroit, the Bears led 13-3 in the fourth quarter. Then Chicago's defense and special teams gave up an NFL record 34 points in the fourth quarter, and the Bears lost 37-27. Against the Vikings, Griese threw for 381 yards, but the defense was again horrible, missing tackles left and right. Rookie Viking running back Adrian Peterson rushed for 224 yards, the most ever allowed by the Bears to one player in a game. The once fearsome Chicago defense allowed 311 total yards rushing in the game.

Some people blamed overconfidence for the Bears' poor defensive performance. Brian Urlacher disagreed. "Last year's over," the middle linebacker said. "This is a different team, a different season, that's all there is to it. We just haven't played as well."

THE INJURIES BEGIN TO MOUNT

It was not a good year for Brian Urlacher either. The 2007 season was his eighth year in professional football, and his body was starting to show the wear and tear of so many games. He found himself playing in pain and beginning to realize that his career would not last forever.

Urlacher's season was extremely erratic. He had 15 tackles in the season-opening loss to the San Diego Chargers and 13 in a dramatic 19-16 victory over the Philadelphia Eagles in Week 7. However, he had just three tackles against Dallas in Week 3 and only five against Minnesota on October 14. It was no secret to anyone that Urlacher's back was bothering him. He sat out a large part of training camp and frequently missed practices.

In the eighth game of the season, the Bears lost to the Detroit Lions, 16-7. After the game, Urlacher admitted that he was having trouble bending down and backpedaling, and had recently seen a specialist in Pittsburgh. The doctors called it an arthritic back. "The thing that's so frustrating," Urlacher said, "is there is no clear-cut solution to give me relief. I just have to deal with the pain."

Urlacher's back was clearly bothering him. He grew increasingly sensitive to media criticism of his performance and often limited his responses to a couple of words. "The pain is actually worse than when I tore my hamstring a couple of years ago," he told the press. "It prevents me from bending, and if I can't bend, I'm not able to be as athletic. I also can't backpedal like I need to. . . . The frustrating thing is they can't pinpoint it exactly so I have no idea when it will hurt or hold me back, but the pain is pretty much always there." In addition, he was feeling unrelated pain in his lower neck and arm that was not helped by throwing himself headfirst into running backs and quarterbacks.

Still, with a fantastic finish, Urlacher had one of his most statistically productive seasons in 2007. In the last five games, Urlacher recorded 52 tackles, two sacks, four interceptions, and one fumble recovery. He returned one of those interceptions 85 yards for a touchdown in a 35-7 rout of the Packers at the end of the season. It was the first interception return for a touchdown of his career and was particularly satisfying to Urlacher since the Packers were 12–2 at the time. The Bears' middle linebacker finished with 123 tackles, essentially the same number as in his Defensive Player of the Year season.

Despite the injuries, he started all 16 games at middle linebacker for the third consecutive season and sixth time in his career. For the season, Urlacher had a career-high five interceptions and led the Bears, an unusual feat for a linebacker. Added to his three interceptions in 2006, Urlacher had eight interceptions in two seasons, the most by an NFL linebacker. However, he failed to make the Pro Bowl for only the second time since 2000 and the first time while playing a full season.

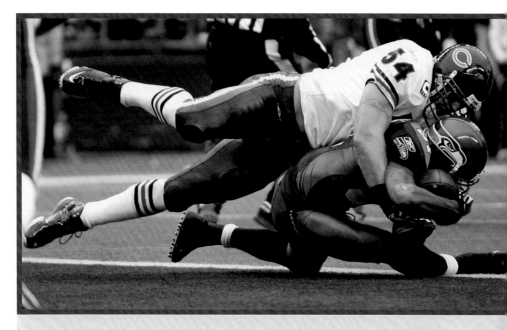

The years of physical abuse from playing professional football began to affect Urlacher's performance. He was often absent in training due to a bad back and was in pain throughout much of the 2007 season.

A NEW CONTRACT

In January 2008, Urlacher underwent neck surgery to try to ease the pain in his lower neck that affected the curve of his cervical spine. He would be 30 years old in May, and the greater part of his career was behind him. Seeing that the end was drawing near, Urlacher decided to try to renegotiate his contract to add one more guaranteed year and a signing bonus up front.

Urlacher had signed a nine-year contract for $56.5 million in 2003. He now argued that he had outperformed that contract. He was a six-time Pro Bowl performer who was the NFL's Defensive Player of the Year in 2005, yet he was only the ninth-highest-paid player on the Bears in 2007.

Urlacher's desire for more money did not go down well with the fans in Chicago. "It's easy for people to criticize me for wanting [a new deal], and I understand that it's a contract and I signed it," Urlacher said. "When I signed my deal, the salary cap was $75 million. It's, what, $116 million now? Things have changed." Urlacher tried to explain his point of view: "I understand that all of this, to a normal person, sounds crazy. It's all relative to what you do. If you're a chair-builder, and you feel you're the best at what you do, and other chair-builders are making more than you, then you'd want to be paid more, too."

The Bears, however, were hesitant to renegotiate and give big money to an eight-year veteran who had severe back pain in 2007 and missed the Pro Bowl. Urlacher argued that he was not a health risk. "In my mind, my neck is rehabbed and back to normal," he said. "My back is better now than it was at any point last season."

The negotiations between Urlacher and the Bears were often nasty. At one point, Urlacher threatened to miss training camp. In July 2008, the Bears gave in and signed Urlacher to a new contract with a one-year extension. He would receive a $6 million signing bonus, get a $7.5 million season added in 2012, and have $1 million tacked on to his salaries annually from 2008 to 2011.

ANOTHER DISAPPOINTING SEASON

The Bears finished the roller-coaster 2008 season with a 9–7 record. Chicago still had a shot at the play-offs on the last day of the season but dropped their final game and missed the play-offs for the second consecutive year.

The season began on a high note. In a rematch of Super Bowl XLI, the Bears crushed the Indianapolis Colts on the road in the opening game. They then lost two frustrating games in the fourth quarter, snatching defeat out of the jaws of victory. Against the Carolina Panthers, the Bears led 17-13 in the fourth quarter but failed to convert a fourth-and-1 with less than two minutes remaining. Carolina then drove the field to win the game, 20-17. The next week, Chicago led 24-14 in the fourth quarter, but the Tampa Bay Buccaneer offense, led by Bears castoff Brian Griese, shredded the defense late in the game. Tampa Bay tied the game 24-24 at the end of regulation and won in overtime when the defense again collapsed.

Yet just when prospects looked dismal, the very next week, the Bears' oft-criticized defense stepped up and helped defeat the Philadelphia Eagles, 24-20, with a goal-line stand. So the season went, from low to high and back again. The Bears did win three of their last four games in dramatic style but lost with the season on the line at Houston. If they had beaten the Texans, the Bears would have squeaked into the play-offs as a wild-card team.

If the Bears were hoping for Urlacher to return to greatness in 2008, they were disappointed. He started all 16 games at middle linebacker, but he only made 93 tackles (79 solo). It was the second-lowest total in his career; his worst year was his injury-plagued 2004 season when he only played in nine games. Once again, he failed to make the Pro Bowl. Some people in the Bears organization whispered that his back was still hurting and that he would never again be the same player who had terrorized the NFL in his first seven years.

"HE HAS NEVER FORGOTTEN HIS ROOTS"

Even after he became a football celebrity in Chicago, Urlacher remained attached to his life in Lovington and New Mexico. He has given more than $1 million worth of donations to Lovington High and the University of New Mexico. "I'm just glad UNM gave me a chance," Urlacher said. "If I wouldn't have gotten a scholarship, I probably wouldn't have went to college. I'd be a working man right now."

In January 2009, Urlacher announced a $500,000 cash gift to the UNM football program. "I owe them a lot, and I think I realize that," Urlacher said of the people at UNM. "And those are great guys. Those are the people who shoot you straight." In recognition of the gift, the field at UNM's indoor practice facility now carries his name. At the dedication, Urlacher simply said, "I love the Lobos. . . . New Mexico is the only school that gave me a chance to play football, coming out of Lovington. I'm proud to be a part of this program. I'm proud to say I'm a Lobo."

Urlacher also rewarded Lovington High School for helping him achieve his dreams. After shooting a commercial early in his career, Urlacher donated two $25,000 scholarships to male and female athletes at Lovington. In 2002, he donated $40,000 worth of weightlifting equipment to the school. "I was happy to make this equipment donation," Urlacher said. "Lovington helped shape my football career." He has also paid for better locker rooms, contributed money to a senior after-graduation trip to Lubbock, and bought athletic shoes for every team at the school. The high school football coach said that Urlacher was "one of the kindest human beings I've ever met. He has never forgotten his roots."

Every summer, Urlacher returns to New Mexico to conduct a football camp, during which hundreds of young players get to practice football and meet Urlacher. Every spring, he returns with several NFL players for a charity basketball game in the high school gym. "The money hasn't changed him," said one of his old coaches, Jaime Quiñones. "He's still well-grounded. He hasn't forgotten where he came from. He's still low-key, humble, and very giving."

Urlacher has a genuine soft spot for children. He has given both time and money to the Special Olympics, an organization that helps children with intellectual disabilities develop self-confidence by playing sports. Every year Urlacher buys a large block of season tickets to each Bears home game and gives them out to children from the Special Olympics. In 2002, Urlacher went on the television game show *Wheel of Fortune* and won $47,000. He split the money between Special Olympics groups in New Mexico and Illinois.

Urlacher believes his success would not have been possible without the support and assistance of his high school and university, and he frequently makes donations to both places. In honor of his achievements and contributions, Lovington has painted a mural of their hometown hero on South Main Street.

THE CUSTODY BATTLE DRAGS ON

While Urlacher was contributing time and money to the Special Olympics, he was having trouble spending time with his own children. In September 2006, Laurie Urlacher moved out of the big house in Lake Bluff near the Bears' headquarters and back to Arizona. The "stable home" that Urlacher had described in his petition for custody of Kennedy (his son by Tyna Robertson) was now frequently an empty nest. Urlacher lived alone while maintaining the demanding schedule of a pro football player with practices, workouts, meetings, and travel.

The custody and visitation battles between Urlacher and Robertson became more heated. The two battled in court over Kennedy's transportation for visitation. Then, Robertson made public a series of text messages allegedly sent by Urlacher.

According to court papers, Urlacher called her "a hooker" and used various other descriptive obscenities. Urlacher never denied sending the messages, saying only that he did not remember.

In 2008, Urlacher was back in an Illinois court fighting over custody arrangements for Kennedy, now three years old. Robertson threatened to block Urlacher's visitation unless he agreed to stop painting Kennedy's toenails blue and putting the boy in pink diapers. Robertson claimed that these behaviors were confusing the child as to his gender. Once again, Urlacher's private life became talk-show comedy. Meanwhile, he continued to try to gain maximum access to all his children. "They're everything to me," he said. "If this [fame and fortune] all went away tomorrow, I'd be fine as long as I had them."

In 2008, Urlacher purchased a home in Chandler, a Phoenix suburb, so that he could be closer to his daughters. "The hardest part is being away from them," he said. "The girls, I see them about every two, three weeks during the season, which is hard. And I'm away from my son three weeks a month. You can see I'm a much happier person when I'm around my kids."

DISLOCATED WRIST

Urlacher started the 2009 season in an optimistic mood. He was happy with his contract extension from the previous year and determined to show he was worth the money. Even better, the Bears had finally acquired a capable quarterback by trading for Pro Bowl quarterback Jay Cutler. Urlacher said that he felt great and that his back and neck were healthier than they had been for two years. "This is the best position we've been in since I've been here," he said. "Obviously, our quarterback situation is pretty stinking good right now. If we just stay healthy, play consistently, I don't see why we can't go to the Super Bowl."

The first game of the 2009 season was against the hated Green Bay Packers, and Urlacher looked like his old self. In the first quarter, he delivered a crunching hit on Aaron Rodgers just as the Packers quarterback released a pass downfield. With about four minutes left in the quarter, Urlacher tackled a running back and Packers guard Josh Sitton accidentally landed on him at the end of the play. Urlacher thought his right wrist was jammed; he got up and briefly shook his wrist before walking

THE BRIAN PICCOLO AWARD

The Brian Piccolo Award is named for former Chicago Bears running back Brian Piccolo, who died of cancer at age 26. Piccolo joined the Bears in 1965 as an undrafted free agent even though he led the nation with 111 points and 1,044 yards rushing at Wake Forest University. He was in his fourth NFL season when a chest X-ray revealed that he had cancer. Piccolo died several months later. His life and his courageous struggle with cancer were later portrayed in the classic movie *Brian's Song*.

The Brian Piccolo Award is given annually to the Chicago Bear who shows he has the same qualities that made Piccolo a great person—loyalty, dedication, teamwork, and a sense of humor. In 2008, Urlacher became only the fifth player to win the Piccolo Award as a rookie and as a veteran. "It's a wonderful award to be a part of because it's a chance we get as teammates to honor one another," Urlacher said. "They're the guys I'm out there playing with every day, going to practice with, and I appreciate their vote."

When Piccolo died, his particular type of cancer was 100 percent fatal, but the cure rate today is 95 percent. Proceeds from the Brian Piccolo Cancer Research Fund benefit research for breast cancer and the developmentally disabled. The fund has raised more than $5 million since 1991.

away with what looked like nothing more than a minor injury. He already had three tackles in the first quarter, and his tenth season was off to a good start. And then it was over.

Urlacher kept playing with the pain until halftime. In the locker room, doctors discovered that he had dislocated his right lunate bone, one of the eight bones of the wrist and one of the most important in terms of the function of the arm and hand. Urlacher wanted to keep playing, but his season was gone. "Talk about a guy that's a great leader," said Hunter Hillenmeyer, who replaced Urlacher at middle linebacker. "First, he plays an entire half of football with a dislocated wrist. I don't think there's many people who can do something like that."

When the Bears arrived at the airport in Chicago around 1:30 A.M. on Monday, an ambulance was waiting in the landing area to rush Urlacher to the hospital. At 3:00 A.M., doctors performed surgery on his wrist. The bone was completely displaced, so surgeons had to pin it back into place with five pins and then fix all the ligaments. The Bears placed Urlacher on injured reserve for the remainder of the season. Head coach Lovie Smith commented that Urlacher "had put himself in position to have an outstanding year. He was playing well in the game before he went down with the injury. Even after the injury to his hand, the competitor in him wanted to continue to play. It's a tough break."

Some fans wanted Urlacher to play against doctors' orders with his wrist in a hard cast. Urlacher thought that idea was a sick joke. "If I could play, I would, I'll tell you that much," he said. "I can't even start rehab for three months. My arm is bent permanently right now, and the cast is up to my biceps. If the doctors thought it was safe enough for me to play, they would let me play. But it's not. So I can't." To say Urlacher was frustrated was an understatement. He got a laugh when he said, "I just wish it would have been my left hand so I can play Ping-Pong and video games. I can't even tie my shoes right now." The pins would be removed in eight weeks. "I think the tough part is letting it sit these eight weeks," he said. "I can do the elliptical machine, stuff with my legs." He vowed, "I'm positive this is not going to mess up my career. It's going to heal. I'm going to do my rehab. And I'll be ready for the off-season."

Meanwhile, the Bears' defense was seeing some dark days, finishing the season twenty-first in points allowed. The low point was a 45-10 loss to the Cincinnati Bengals—the most points Chicago had ever surrendered during the Lovie Smith era. The Bengals scored on their first seven possessions and racked up 448 yards against the Chicago defense. To make matters worse, Cedric Benson, a former Bear, ran for a career-high 189 yards. The Bears had not been so humiliated since Dick Jauron's team lost the 2003 season opener, 49-7, at San Francisco. They finished the 2009 season that had begun with such high hopes at a mediocre 7–9. The Bears' record was now 7–17 in games that Urlacher did not start at middle linebacker.

QUESTIONS

In 2008, Urlacher said, "When I first came into the league, I said I wanted to play 10 years," he said. "Now I think I can play 12 or 13. . . . I don't want to be an old guy, trying to play with these young guys, who can't keep up anymore. I'll know when it's time for that. But I'm not close to that right now."

However, 2008 had not been a great year for him. "What am I proud of from last season?" Urlacher asked. "I didn't have any sacks. I only had two picks. There's not a lot to be proud of when you're 9–7 and don't go to the play-offs. I just have to get better. . . . I just have to be more physical at the point of attack. . . . I've got to get back to where I was a few years ago when I was just downhill attacking, hitting people in the mouth—offensive linemen, fullbacks, everybody."

Then came the wrist injury. It's one thing to vow to return better than ever. It's a different matter to be 32 years old with an arthritic back, a surgically repaired neck, and the wear and tear of nine seasons playing middle linebacker in the NFL. Urlacher had not played consistently at an elite level since the Bears went to Super Bowl XLI following the 2006 season.

Would Urlacher really be able to come back in 2010? Some people did not think so. In October 2007, Urlacher had signed a four-year contract with a company that paid him $275,000 a year to use his likeness and sell autographed memorabilia. After Urlacher hurt his wrist, the company tried to get out of the contract, claiming that the Bears' star had suffered a career-ending injury. Urlacher immediately sued the company, claiming that it just wanted to get out of the contract.

Urlacher had been durable for most of his career except for the 2004 season. Before the 2009 season, Urlacher said that he was in great shape. The wrist injury was a freak injury, not related to his back or neck. Maybe the year off would be a blessing in disguise?

REDEMPTION

When Urlacher showed up for training camp in 2010, he was a bit nervous for perhaps the first time since his rookie year. He hadn't hit anybody at full speed or in pads since the injury in the Green Bay game a year before. Would he still be able to play at age 32 after so much time off?

The answers weren't long in coming. "I wasn't worried about my wrist after the first couple days of training camp," Urlacher said. "I felt pretty good about it, and the rest of my body felt great." In a weird way, the injury had a silver lining. Urlacher admitted that the time away from football had allowed him to heal his body and recharge his mind.

Nonetheless, not much was expected of the Bears when the 2010 season began. Those low expectations seemed to be confirmed when they fell to 4–3 heading into their bye week. The team, though, began to run the ball more frequently, and the pieces just seemed to fall into place. The Bears won seven of their last nine games and clinched a play-off spot with two games remaining.

The resurgence was certainly not down to the offense, which finished a pathetic 30th out of 32 NFL teams in total yards gained. Although quarterback Jay Cutler occasionally had strong games, and running back Matt Forte rushed for more than 1,000 yards, return specialist Devin Hester remained the main offensive threat. Hester returned three punts for touchdowns, setting the NFL record for return touchdowns in a career.

Instead, the Bears' success was once again based on their defense and the strong play of Brian Urlacher. Urlacher was helped by the preseason acquisition of Pro Bowl defensive end Julius Peppers. The Bears lured the free-agent Peppers from the Carolina Panthers with a six-year, $91.5 million contract. For this season, at least, he was worth the money. Peppers was a force all over the field, pressuring opposing quarterbacks, redirecting running plays, and assisting on tackles. Peppers and defensive end Israel Idonije both finished the season with eight sacks. Cornerback Charles Tillman and safety Chris Harris each had five interceptions, and linebacker Lance Briggs was second on the team with 113 tackles.

Healthy and rejuvenated, Urlacher's play was back to near his best. At 32, he started all 16 games, leading the Bears with 125 total tackles, the third-highest total of his career (behind 2002 and 2006). He also registered 96 solo tackles, four sacks, and an interception. He had lost a step or two over the years and was no longer the 4.59 closer of his younger years. But 10 years in the NFL was a lot of experience, and Urlacher tried to compensate with intelligence for what he had lost in age and wear and tear.

"He's got a time machine somewhere because he dialed it back three or four years, and he's playing at a really high level," Detroit Lions coach Jim Schwartz said. "I don't know if there's a middle linebacker playing at a higher level in the NFL." Midway through the season, Urlacher broke Mike Singletary's career franchise record for tackles. "He's been all over the field making plays, back to his old self," safety Chris Harris said. "He's the leader on this team."

In December, Urlacher led the NFC with 49 tackles, including 17 in a loss to the New England Patriots and 11 in a win over the Detroit Lions. For his efforts, Urlacher was named NFC Defensive Player of the Month for December. Amazingly, it was the first time he had ever won the award in his career.

With Urlacher and the defense leading the way, the Bears improved to an 11–5 record in 2010. Chicago won the NFC North, their first division title since 2006, and earned a first-round bye for the 2011 play-offs. Chicago's defense, ranked twenty-third against the run in 2009, rebounded to rank fourth in 2010. Briggs, Peppers, and Urlacher all made the Pro Bowl. For the often unsung Briggs, it was a particularly rewarding honor—his sixth consecutive Pro Bowl. He was only the fourth linebacker in Bears history to be selected to six straight Pro Bowls, joining the illustrious company of Dick Butkus, Bill George, and Mike Singletary. For Urlacher, it was his seventh Pro Bowl, but his first since the 2006 season. To cap it all off, Peppers finished fourth and Urlacher fifth in the voting for the 2010 Defensive Player of the Year.

2011 PLAY-OFFS

Perhaps the only ill omen was the fact that the Bears were scheduled to play their hated rivals, the Green Bay Packers, in the last week of the season. It was a meaningless game for the Bears, but the Packers needed a victory to make the play-offs. Many people wondered if the Bears would play their starters or rest them to avoid the possibility of unnecessary injuries. Coach Smith decided to play most of his starters, but the Bears lost 10-3, granting the dangerous Packers entry into the postseason.

In the first round of the NFC play-offs, the Seattle Seahawks, with the worst record for a play-off team in NFL history (7–9), shocked the defending NFL champion New Orleans Saints in a 41-36 victory. This win, combined with the Packers' victory over the Eagles in Philadelphia, brought Seattle to Chicago and allowed Green Bay to play the top-seeded Falcons in Atlanta.

Twice in Brian Urlacher's career, the Bears had thrown away the play-off bye and the home-field advantage and lost play-off games they were favored to win. This time, however, the Bears pounded the Seahawks from the beginning of the game on a snowy field in Chicago. Quarterback Jay Cutler ran for two touchdowns and threw for two, including a 58-yard touchdown pass to Greg Olsen on Chicago's third offensive play. The Bears built a 28-0 lead and cruised to a 35-24 victory over the Seahawks.

As fate would have it, the Packers won their second straight postseason road victory, a stunning 48-21 rout of the Falcons. This brought Green Bay to Chicago for a dream NFC Championship Game, with the winner going to the Super Bowl. It was probably the biggest game in the 90-year series between the Packers and the Bears. It would be the one hundred eighty-second time the two teams played, but their first-ever meeting for the NFC title. In fact, it would be the first play-off meeting between the bitter rivals since the Bears beat the Packers in 1941, a week after the bombing of Pearl Harbor.

A week of unprecedented hype preceded the game. Fans of both teams declared in all seriousness that the game was "bigger than the Super Bowl" and that winning it meant more to them than the NFL championship. "It's a big deal. We have a lot of history with them," Urlacher said. "We don't like them, they don't like us." Even though the game was at Soldier Field and the Bears had a better record, bookmakers made the Packers 3½ point favorites.

As many people expected, Chicago's offense was sluggish all game. In the previous 20 years, the Bears had started 23 different quarterbacks, while the Packers had started three in the same stretch. This NFC Championship Game turned out to be a microcosm of that amazing statistic, as the Bears ended the

Coming back from a dislocated wrist, Urlacher helped the Bears trounce the Seattle Seahawks in the 2011 NFC play-offs (*above*). Although they did not win the NFC championship that year, many believe that Urlacher still has the potential to lead the Bears into future victories.

game with their third-string quarterback nearly rallying them to victory.

Jay Cutler, the starting quarterback, was consistently off target. He completed only 6 of 14 passes for 80 yards and an interception. His poor performance was partially caused by a nasty left knee injury in the second quarter when Cutler sprained his medial collateral ligament (MCL), which helps stabilize the knee joint. He tried to return in the second half, but it was impossible for him to continue, and he was ruled out of the game by Chicago's medical staff.

The seldom-used backup quarterback, Todd Collins, lasted only two possessions. He was then replaced by third-stringer Caleb Hanie, an undrafted free agent out of Colorado State in 2008. Incredibly, Hanie revived the Bears offense and led them to a touchdown. With about six minutes to go, however, Hanie was intercepted by 330-pound (150-kilogram) B.J. Raji, who returned the ball 18 yards for a touchdown to give the Packers a 21-7 lead. It turned out Green Bay needed the points. Minutes after throwing the interception, Hanie threw a 35-yard touchdown pass to Earl Bennett with 4:43 left. In the 81-second drive, Hanie went 4-for-4 for 60 yards.

Amazingly, the Chicago defense held, and the Bears got the ball back again. It looked as though it might be a storybook ending for Chicago, as Hanie tried to lead them to their third touchdown of the fourth quarter. Unfortunately for Bears fans, it was not to be. With a fourth down deep in Packer territory, and less than two minutes remaining to play, Sam Shields intercepted Hanie at the Packers' 12-yard line to end the Bears' Super Bowl dreams. The final score of the NFC Championship Game was Packers 21, Bears 14.

In the midst of all their offensive woes, the Bears' defense in general, and Brian Urlacher in particular, kept Chicago in the game in the second half. The defense gave up only 14 points in the game (the other touchdown was Raji's interception) and held the Packers to 1-for-8 on third downs in the final 30 minutes. Chicago gave up only 104 total yards after halftime, after being ripped for 252 in the first half.

Urlacher had a monster game, recording a game-high nine solo tackles, including two for losses. He sacked Packers quarterback Aaron Rodgers once for eight yards and deflected a pass. Urlacher also made the defensive calls and alignments that kept the Bears in the game while the offense struggled.

Urlacher's most important, yet most frustrating, play came when he intercepted Rodgers on Green Bay's first drive of the third quarter. The Packers were at the Bears' 6, threatening to increase their lead to 21-0, when Urlacher stepped in front of Rodgers's pass. He returned it 33 yards before Rodgers, the last man, took out his legs and prevented a touchdown. If Urlacher still had his old speed, Rodgers would never have caught him and he would have returned it for a touchdown. As it was, Urlacher's interception not only kept the Bears alive but also revived the home crowd of 62,000 after a dismal first half.

"It's a disappointing way to end the season," Urlacher said after the loss. "It's not the way I wanted to end it. But, you know, no one expected us to be here, we know that. . . . [Yet it] doesn't make it any easier for us to lose this game. We expected to win this game, we expected to play good." As fan Roy Taylor said, "While the Bears' 2010 season turned out breathtakingly exciting for its followers, in the end the team lost out in the worst way it possibly could. . . . Losing at home in the NFC Championship to your most hated rival certainly has to be the worst way to go down."

WHAT THE FUTURE MAY HOLD

"We're in this for the long haul," Lance Briggs said. "We might have fallen short of our goal this year. But next year, we won't fall short." The immediate future, however, was bleak for Urlacher, the Bears, and their fans. Their hated archrivals, the Green Bay Packers, went to the Super Bowl and defeated the Pittsburgh Steelers, 31-25. It was a bitter pill for Bears fans to swallow. As always, Urlacher had the most entertaining sound bite. When asked if he would root for Green Bay, he avoided the usual bland "nonquote" often associated with athletes. "Hell, no. I'm not rooting for the Packers in the Super Bowl," Urlacher said. "I have a ton of respect for that organization and the head coach, but I don't want them to win the Super Bowl. They're in our division; I want them to lose."

In the longer term, Urlacher's future was unclear. The 2010 season was his best in years, but the season he took off because of the wrist injury probably played a big factor in Urlacher's resurgence. He seemed to end 2010 in excellent condition, but he turned 33 in May 2011. That's an age when Hall of Fame linebackers start to think about retiring. Dick Butkus only played 9 years; Willie Lanier and Jack Lambert, 11; Mike Singletary and Sam Huff, 12; Harry Carson and Lawrence Taylor, 13. No one can play forever. For Urlacher, 2010 was his eleventh season in the NFL.

Yet, it seems unlikely that Urlacher would retire after such a stellar season with a Bears team that made the play-offs. So maybe there are chapters still to be written in Brian Urlacher's biography.

STATISTICS

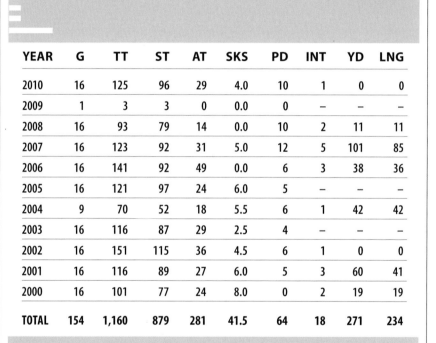

BRIAN URLACHER
POSITION: Middle linebacker

FULL NAME: Brian Keith Urlacher

BORN: May 25, 1978, Pasco, Washington

HEIGHT: 6'4"

WEIGHT: 258 lbs.

COLLEGE: University of New Mexico

TEAM: Chicago Bears (2000–)

YEAR	G	TT	ST	AT	SKS	PD	INT	YD	LNG
2010	16	125	96	29	4.0	10	1	0	0
2009	1	3	3	0	0.0	0	–	–	–
2008	16	93	79	14	0.0	10	2	11	11
2007	16	123	92	31	5.0	12	5	101	85
2006	16	141	92	49	0.0	6	3	38	36
2005	16	121	97	24	6.0	5	–	–	–
2004	9	70	52	18	5.5	6	1	42	42
2003	16	116	87	29	2.5	4	–	–	–
2002	16	151	115	36	4.5	6	1	0	0
2001	16	116	89	27	6.0	5	3	60	41
2000	16	101	77	24	8.0	0	2	19	19
TOTAL	**154**	**1,160**	**879**	**281**	**41.5**	**64**	**18**	**271**	**234**

CHRONOLOGY

1978   Brian Urlacher is born on May 25 in Pasco, Washington.

1986   Lavoyda Urlacher moves family to Lovington, New Mexico, after her divorce.

1992   Lavoyda Urlacher marries Troy Lenard.

1995   Brian leads Lovington High School to Class 3A New Mexico football championship.

1996–2000   Attends the University of New Mexico in Albuquerque.

1998   Chosen first-team All-Western Athletic Conference as a junior.

Leads NCAA in tackles.

1999   Recognized as AP First-Team All-American.

Wins Mountain West Conference Player of the Year.

2000   Chosen by the Chicago Bears with the ninth pick in the first round of NFL Draft.

Leads Bears in tackles.

Wins AP NFL Defensive Rookie of the Year.

Marries Laurie Faulhaber.

Daughter Pamela Urlacher is born.

2001   Wins *Football Digest* NFL Defensive Player of the Year.

Finishes fifth in NFL MVP voting.

Bears lose in first round of the play-offs.

2002   Records a career-high 151 tackles; breaks Bears all-time record.

2003   Signs nine-year contract worth $56.65 million.

2004   Divorces Laurie Urlacher.

Plays only nine games because of injuries.

2005   Wins AP NFL Defensive Player of the Year.

Daughter Riley Urlacher is born.

Son Kennedy Urlacher is born.

Bears lose in first round of the play-offs.

2006–2007   Leads Chicago to 13–3 record and the NFC championship.

Bears lose 29-14 to the Indianapolis Colts in Super Bowl XLI.

2007   Intercepts career-high five passes in season.

2008   Renegotiates contract, with a one-year extension.

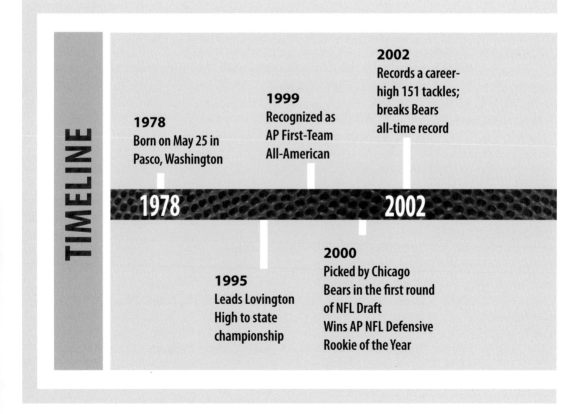

TIMELINE

1978
Born on May 25 in
Pasco, Washington

1999
Recognized as
AP First-Team
All-American

2002
Records a career-
high 151 tackles;
breaks Bears
all-time record

1978   2002

1995
Leads Lovington
High to state
championship

2000
Picked by Chicago
Bears in the first round
of NFL Draft
Wins AP NFL Defensive
Rookie of the Year

Recovers career-high four fumbles in season.

2009   Dislocates wrist in first game; misses rest of the season.

2010   Makes 125 tackles in comeback season.

Leads Chicago to 11–5 record.

Bears defeat Seattle Seahawks 35-24 in the divisional round of the play-offs.

Bears lose to the Green Bay Packers, 21-14, in the NFC Championship Game.

2005
Wins AP NFL Defensive Player of the Year

2009
Dislocates wrist in first game; misses rest of the season

2003

2010

2003
Signs nine-year contract worth $56.65 million

2007
Bears lose to the Colts in Super Bowl XLI

2010
Makes 125 tackles in comeback season

BRIAN URLACHER

GLOSSARY

audible A play called by the quarterback or the defensive play caller at the line of scrimmage to change the play called in the huddle. Brian Urlacher usually calls the defensive audibles for the Bears.

backup A second-string player who does not start the game but comes in later in relief of a starter.

blitz A defensive maneuver in which one or more linebackers or defensive backs, who normally remain behind the line of scrimmage, instead charge into the opponent's backfield.

block The act of obstructing a defensive player's path with an offensive player's body.

center A player position on offense; a center snaps the ball to the quarterback to start the play.

cornerback A defensive back who lines up near the line of scrimmage across from a wide receiver. The cornerback's main job is to disrupt passing routes, to defend against passers, and to contain running plays. Most defensive formations use two cornerbacks.

custody The authority given to one or both parents by a court to make major decisions regarding the child. One parent (sole custody) or both parents (joint custody) may have custody. Urlacher has often been involved in custody battles.

defensive back A cornerback or safety position on the defensive team. Defensive backs commonly defend against wide receivers on passing plays. There are usually four defensive backs playing at a time.

defensive end A player on defense who lines up on the outside of the defensive line. Most defensive formations use two defensive ends.

defensive tackle A player on defense on the inside of the defensive line whose main function is to contain the run.

Defensive tackles are usually the largest defensive players on the field.

draft   The selection of collegiate players for entrance into the National Football League. Typically, the team with the worst record in the previous season picks first in the draft. Urlacher was the ninth pick in the 2000 NFL Draft.

drive   A continuous set of offensive plays gaining substantial yardage and several first downs, usually leading to a scoring opportunity.

end zone   The area between the end line and the goal line (10 yards), bounded by the sidelines.

field goal   A scoring play of three points made by placekicking or drop-kicking the ball through the goalposts in the opponent's end zone.

first down   The first of a set of four downs. Usually, a team that has a first down needs to advance the ball 10 yards to receive another first down.

formation   An arrangement of the offensive or defensive players.

free agent   A professional player who is not under contract with any football team and may sign with any team he chooses.

fumble   When an offensive player loses possession of the ball before the end of the play.

guard   A player position on the offensive line. Most teams use two guards on either side of the center. They are blocking specialists.

handoff   The act of giving the ball to another player during an offensive play. It generally occurs when the quarterback hands the ball to a running back.

Heisman Trophy   An award presented annually to the most outstanding player in Division I-A college football.

holding   A penalty that occurs when one player keeps another from advancing by grabbing him and holding him back. Offensive holding is a 10-yard penalty, and the down is repeated. Defensive holding results in a 5-yard penalty and an automatic first down.

huddle   An on-field gathering of members of a team to secretly communicate instructions for the next play.

interception   An offensive pass that is caught by the defensive player, giving his team the ball.

linebacker   A player position on defense. Linebackers typically play slightly behind the defensive linemen. Most defenses use either three or four linebackers.

line of scrimmage   The imaginary line that stretches across the field and separates the two teams before the ball is snapped. Before a play, the offensive and defensive teams line up on opposite sides of the line of scrimmage.

National Football League (NFL)   The largest American football league, with 32 franchise teams.

offensive line   The five offensive players (usually a center, two guards, and two tackles) who line up on the line of scrimmage. Their primary job is to block the defensive players, and they almost never touch the football.

penalty   A punishment for breaking the rules.

Pro Bowl   The all-star game of the NFL, played after the season ends. As of 2011, players were voted to the Pro Bowl by coaches, fellow players, and fans.

punt   A kick in which the ball is dropped and kicked before it reaches the ground. It is usually used to give the ball to the opposition on fourth down. Urlacher returned punts in high school and college.

quarterback   The offensive player who receives the ball from the center at the start of each play. The quarterback will hand off the ball, pass the ball, or run it himself. It is the most visible position in football.

reception   When an offensive player catches (receives) a pass.

rookie   A player's first year as a professional.

running back   An offensive player who runs with the football; also known as a tailback, halfback, or fullback.

sack   When a defensive player tackles a ball carrier (usually a quarterback) who intends to throw a forward pass.

safety   A player position on defense. Safeties are defensive backs and usually the last line of defense. Most defensive teams play with two safeties ("free" and "strong"). Urlacher played free safety in college.

salary cap   A limit on the amount an NFL team can spend on its players' salaries. The NFL introduced the salary cap in 1994 to bring parity to the NFL and limit players' wages.

sideline   One of the lines marking each side of the football field.

starter   A player who is the first to play his position within a given game or season.

tackle   The act of forcing a ballcarrier to the ground.

tight end   An offensive player who lines up on the line of scrimmage next to the offensive tackle. Tight ends are used as blockers on running plays. On pass plays, they help block the defense or run a passing route.

touchdown   A play worth 6 points in which any part of the ball, while legally in the possession of the player, crosses the plane of the opponent's goal line. A touchdown allows the team that scored a choice for 1 extra point by kicking the ball through the goalposts or for 2 extra points by running or passing the ball into the end zone.

turnover   The loss of possession of the ball by one team to the other team, usually resulting from a fumble or an interception.

wide receiver   A player position on offense. He is split wide (about 10 yards) from the formation and plays on the line of scrimmage as a split end or a yard off the line of scrimmage as a flanker.

wild card   The two NFL play-off spots given to the two non-division-winning teams that have the best record in each conference.

BIBLIOGRAPHY

BOOKS

Brian Urlacher: Windy City Warrior. Champaign, Ill.: Sports Publishing, 2002.

Levy, Marv. *Marv Levy: Where Else Would You Rather Be?* Champaign, Ill.: Sports Publishing, 2004.

McCambridge, Michael. *America's Game: The Epic Story of How Pro Football Captured a Nation.* New York: Random House, 2004.

Oriard, Michael. *Brand NFL: Making and Selling America's Favorite Sport.* Chapel Hill: University of North Carolina Press, 2007.

Sandler, Michael. *Brian Urlacher (Football Heroes Making a Difference).* New York: Bearport, 2009.

Savage, Jeff. *Brian Urlacher.* Minneapolis, Minn.: Lerner Publications, 2010.

Uschan, Michael. *Brian Urlacher (Superstars of Pro Football).* Broomall, Pa.: Mason Crest, 2009.

ARTICLES AND WEB SITES

"Anatomy of a Fine." *Sports Illustrated,* April 30, 2007. Available online. URL: http://sportsillustrated.cnn.com/vault/article/magazine/MAG1110931/1/index.htm.

Anderson, Dave. "There's No Shuffle in His Step." *New York Times,* February 1, 2007.

Archuleta, Greg. "A Bear Among Boys: Urlacher's Camp Draws Record Number of Kids." *Albuquerque Journal,* June 27, 2007.

———. "Personal Growth." *Albuquerque Journal,* October 9, 1998.

Armour, Nancy. "Soft-spoken Guy Named Lovie Is Perfect Fit for Bears." NBC Sports, November 4, 2006. Available online. URL: http://nbcsports.msnbc.com/id/15534044/.

Associated Press. "Bears LB Urlacher Playing with Arthritis in Back." ESPN.com, October 28, 2007. Available online. URL: http://sports.espn.go.com/nfl/news/story?id=3084394.

Associated Press. "NFL Fines Urlacher $100K for Super Bowl Hat." ESPN.com, April 20, 2007. Available online. URL: http://sports.espn.go.com/nfl/news/story?id=2841997.

"Bears Get First Division Title in 11 Years." CBC News, January 6, 2002. Available online. URL: http://www.cbc.ca/sports/story/2002/01/06/bears020105.html.

"Bears Show Offense That Was Missing During Jauron Era." CBS Sports, October 8, 2006. Available online. URL: http://www.cbssports.com/nfl/gamecenter/recap/NFL_20061008_BUF@CHI.

"Bears' Urlacher Will Miss Rest of Season with Dislocated Wrist." SI.com, September 14, 2009.

Beilue, Jon Mark. " '75 Big Sandy: Legendary Team Was a Handful." *Amarillo Globe-News*, December 14, 2005. Available online. URL: http://www.amarillo.com/stories/121405/hss_3487166.shtml.

Biggs, Brad. "Bears Have to Weigh Dollars with Urlacher." Nationalfootballpost.com, September 15, 2009.

———. "Bears Humiliated By Benson, Bengals." *Chicago Sun-Times*, October 26, 2009.

"Big Plays Highlighted Productive Season for Urlacher." Chicagobears.com, January 27, 2008. Available online. URL: http://www.chicagobears.com/news/NewsStory.asp?story_id=4323.

"Bills Get EmBEARassed, 5-0 Record." Chicagobears.com,
October 12, 2006. Available online. URL: http://www.
gamespot.com/pages/unions/read_article.php?topic_
id=25054677&union_id=8170.

Boeck, Greg. "Bear Country in New Mexico: Urlacher's Roots
Run Deep in Home Town." *USA Today,* January 28, 2007.
Available online. URL: http://www.usatoday.com/sports/
football/nfl/bears/2007-01-28-brian-urlacher-cover_x.htm.

"Brian Urlacher." NFL.com. Available online at http://www.nfl
.com/players/brianurlacher/careerstats?id=URL059326.

"Brian Urlacher." JockBio.com, 2007. Available online. URL:
http://www.jockbio.com/Bios/Urlacher/Urlacher_bio.html.

"Brian Urlacher 'Big Hits, Big Plays.'" VodPod. Available online.
URL: http://vodpod.com/watch/1949-brian-urlacher-big-
hits-big-plays.

"Brian Urlacher University of New Mexico's Indoor Practice Dedication." New Mexico Overtime Sports Center,
2009. Available online. URL: http://nmotsc.com/articles/
brian-urlacher-university-of-new-mexicos-indoor-practice-
dedication/.

Brown, Clifton. "A Position of Greatness, and a Hunger for
Victory." *New York Times,* January 14, 2007.

Campbell, Steve. "There's No Need to Sugarcoat It Anymore:
Franchione Must Go." *Houston Chronicle,* October 28, 2007.
Available online. URL: http://www.chron.com/disp/story
.mpl/sports/college/texasam/5251825.html.

Chadiha, Jeffri. "N.o. Problem." *Sports Illustrated,* January 22,
2007. Available online. URL: http://sportsillustrated.cnn
.com/vault/article/magazine/MAG1105615/index.htm.

———. "Upwardly Mobile." *Sports Illustrated*, May 8, 2000. Available online. URL: http://sportsillustrated.cnn.com/vault/article/magazine/MAG1019148/index.htm.

"Chicago Bears Franchise Encyclopedia." Pro Football Reference. Available online. URL: http://www.pro-football-reference.com/teams/chi/.

"Chicago Bears History." Available online. URL: http://www.bearshistory.com/source/home.aspx.

"Chicago 27, Cleveland 21." *Sports Illustrated*, November 4, 2001. Available online. URL: http://sportsillustrated.cnn.com/football/nfl/recaps/2001/11/04/bears_browns/.

Costa, Brian, and Kevin Baxter. "Rainy Night Made for Sloppy Game; Fans Weather Storm." *Providence Journal*, February 5, 2007. Available online. URL: http://www.projo.com/sports/content/sp_super_atmosphere05_02-05-07_0E494TD.1e824f6.html.

Dell'Apa, Frank. "Bush Caught Looking Back: Rookie's Taunting Fired Up Chicago." *Boston Globe*, January 22, 2007.

Drehs, Wayne. "Big Sandy Loves Lovie." ESPN.com, January 28, 2007. Available online. URL: http://sports.espn.go.com/nfl/playoffs06/news/story?id=2744049.

"First Person: Brian Urlacher." *Sports Illustrated*, November 9, 2004. Available online. URL: http://sportsillustrated.cnn.com/2004/players/11/09/first_person1115/.

Gano, Rick. "Urlacher: Small Town to the Super Bowl." Associated Press, January 30, 2007. Available online. URL: http://www.pantagraph.com/sports/professional/article_206f5de6-3389-5a89-a75e-fbbc11ab60e2.html.

Hayes, Neil. "With Cutler in Starring Role, Urlacher Era May Be Over." Pro Sports Daily.com, September 15, 2009.

Herrera, Pete. "Urlacher a Throwback to Two-Way Era." *Los Angeles Times*, November 14, 1999. Available online. URL: http://articles.latimes.com/1999/nov/14/sports/sp-33351.

———. "The Urlacher Phenomena Helps Lobos Recruit Chicago Area." *Albuquerque Journal*, February 7, 2007.

"Judge Orders Parenting Class for Bears' Urlacher, Ex-girlfriend." *Albuquerque Journal*, July 12, 2007.

Kirkpatrick, Curry. "Behold Bear Brian Urlacher." *ESPN Magazine*, December 24, 2002. Available online. URL: http://espn.go.com/magazine/vol4no26urlacher.html.

———. "The Next Urlacher." *ESPN Magazine*, December 13, 2001. Available online. URL: http://espn.go.com/magazine/curry_20011212.html.

Konkol, Mark, and Steve Warmbir. "That's Why Gold Digger Doesn't Add Up." *Chicago Sun-Times*, October 29, 2006.

Korte, Tim. "Urlacher Keeps Close to His Roots." *Deseret News*, February 4, 2007. Available online. URL: http://findarticles.com/p/articles/mi_qn4188/is_20070204/ai_n17199782/.

Layden, Tim. "Super Bowl XLI Preview." *Sports Illustrated*, February 5, 2007.

Limón, Iliana. "All About Urlacher." *Albuquerque Tribune*, February 2, 2007. Available online. URL: http://www.abqtrib.com/news/2007/feb/02/monster-connection-all-about-urlacher/.

———. "Younger Urlacher Has No Problem Living in Sibling's Shadow." *Albuquerque Tribune*, February 1, 2007. Available online. URL: http://www.abqtrib.com/news/2007/feb/01/monster-connection-younger-urlacher-has-no-problem/.

"Lovington." New Mexico Tourism Department Web site. Available online. URL: http://www.newmexico.org/explore/regions/southeast/lovington.php#.

Mariotti, Jay. "Put the Chiseler on Hold ..." *Chicago Sun-Times*, April 16, 2000.

———. "Urlacher Insult Cutler? History Says Yes." Fan House, July 29, 2009. Available online. URL: http://jay-mariotti .fanhouse.com/2009/07/29/urlacher-insult-cutler-history-says-yes/.

"Marv Levy's [Hall of Fame] Induction Speech." Pro Football Hall of Fame, August 4, 2001. Available online. URL: http:// www.profootballhof.com/history/release.aspx?release_ id=434.

Mayer, Larry. "Adversity Not Slowing Urlacher's Meteoric Rise." ChicagoBears.com, October 31, 2006. Available online. URL: http://www.chicagobears.com/news/NewsStory .asp?story_id=2603.

———. "Bears Prevail in Overtime, One Win from Super Bowl." ChicagoBears.com, January 14, 2007. Available online. URL: http://www.chicagobears.com/news/NewsStory .asp?story_id=2922.

———. "He's the Randy Moss of Defense." *Football Digest*, March 2001.

———. "Urlacher Admits He's Dealing with Painful Back Injury." ChicagoBears.com, October 28, 2007. Available online. URL: http://www.chicagobears.com/news/ NewsStory.asp?story_id=4021.

———. "Urlacher Feels Injured Teammate Brown's Pain." ChicagoBears.com, September 13, 2007. Available online. URL: http://www.chicagobears.com/news/NewsStory.asp?story_ id=3822.

———. "Urlacher, Olsen Humbled to Receive Piccolo Awards." ProFiles Sports, April 24, 2008. Available online. URL: http:// profilessports.com/Main.aspx?pid=76&tab=77.

McClure, Vaughn. "Brian Urlacher Praises Chicago Bears Medical Team." *Chicago Tribune*, September 20, 2009. Available online. URL: http://articles.chicagotribune.com/2009-09-20/sports/0909190268_1_brian-urlacher-praises-wrist.

———. "Chicago Bears' Defensive Problems More Than Absence of Brian Urlacher." *Chicago Tribune*, November 1, 2009. Available online. URL: http://articles.chicagotribune.com/2009-11-01/sports/0910310278_1_brian-urlacher-hillenmeyer-strong-side-linebacker.

———. "Face It, Brian Urlacher Happy to Take Back Seat to Jay Cutler." *Chicago Tribune*, September 7, 2009. Available online. URL: http://articles.chicagotribune.com/2009-09-07/sports/0909060261_1_brian-urlacher-jay-cutler-lance-briggs.

———. "Urlacher Denies He'll Retire over Contract Dispute." *Star Tribune*, April 19, 2008.

———. "Urlacher Fires Back at Mom of His Son." Chicago Breaking News, November 26, 2008. Available online. URL: http://www.chicagobreakingnews.com/2008/11/urlacher-chicago-bears-nail-polish-diapers.html.

———. "Urlacher Shoots Down Talk of Cutler Insult." *Chicago Tribune*, July 30, 2009. Available online. URL: http://articles.chicagotribune.com/2009-07-30/sports/0907290975_1_brian-urlacher-jay-cutler-wimp.

McKinney, K. "Chicago Bears' Urlacher Back in Court on Custody Case." MyFamilyLaw.com, November 26, 2008. Available online. URL: http://myfamilylaw.com/celebrity-blog/2008/11/26/brian-urlacher-custody-woes/.

"Michael Flatley False Rape Claim: Stripper Faces Jail." *Belfast Telegraph*, December 24, 2008. Available online. URL: http://www.belfasttelegraph.co.uk/news/world-news/michael-flatley-false-rape-claim-stripper-faces-jail-14119804.html.

Moore, Brad. "Brian Urlacher Opens the Final Year of his Stellar Lobo Career as a Top NFL Prospect." Mountain West Conference Web site, September 2, 1999. Available online. URL: http://www.themwc.com/sports/m-footbl/spec-rel/090299aaa.html.

———. "Windy City Messiah." *Albuquerque Tribune*, January 10, 2002. Available online. URL: http://www.abqtrib.com/news/2002/jan/10/windy-city-messiah/?printer=1/.

Mullin, John. "Bears Pull Off Monday Night Miracle." *Chicago Tribune*, October 16, 2006. Available online. URL: http://www.nw32.com/cs-061016bearsgamer,0,2009182.story.

———. "Bump That Got Urlacher Over Hump." *Chicago Tribune*, November 23, 2006. Available online. URL: http://articles.chicagotribune.com/2006-11-23/sports/0611230173_1_brian-urlacher-bears-strong-side-linebacker.

Mullman, Jeremy. "Urlacher's Next Play: Ad Backer; Football Star Flexes Marketing Muscle." *Crain's Chicago Business*, October 7, 2002.

Munson, Lester. "Urlacher Seeks Settlement." SI.com, September 26, 2006. Available online. URL: http://sportsillustrated.cnn.com/2006/writers/lester_munson/09/26/urlacher/index.html.

Murphy, Kevin. "Local Boy Makes Good." *Lubbock Avalanche-Journal*, January 13, 2001. Available online. URL: http://www.lubbockonline.com/stories/011301/pro_011301130.shtml.

New Mexico 2009 Football Media Guide. UNM Media Relations Department, 2009.

"NEXT 2002—Brian Urlacher," *ESPN Magazine*, December 24, 2002 (revised December 7, 2006). Available online. URL:

http://sports.espn.go.com/nfl/playoffs05/sbnext/news/ story?page=sbnext/2002.

"Pro Football 1970." *Sports Illustrated*, September 21, 1970: cover.

Robinson, Jon. "Super Bowl XLI: Brian Urlacher Interview." IGN Sports, January 31, 2007. Available online. URL: http:// sports.ign.com/articles/760/760031p1.html.

Rovell, Darren. "Urlacher's Memorabilia Contract: An Inside Look." CNBC, September 22, 2009. Available online. URL: http://www.cnbc.com/id/32969596.

Shipley, Amy. "Ferocious—in an Understated Way." *Washington Post*, January 31, 2007. Available online. URL: http://www .washingtonpost.com/wp-dyn/content/article/2007/01/30/ AR2007013001616.html.

Silver, Michael. "Middle Management." *Sports Illustrated*, October 29, 2001. Available online. URL: http://sportsillustrated .cnn.com/vault/article/magazine/MAG1024082/3/index .htm#top.

———. "Trippin' Tuesday: Urlacher to Skip Minicamp?" Yahoo! Sports, May 13, 2008. Available online. URL: http://sports .yahoo.com/nfl/news?slug=ms-trippintuesday051308&prov =yhoo&type=lgns.

Silverman, Steve. "The Fire Beneath: Brian Urlacher, a Man of Few Words, Prefers to Let His Tackles Do the Talking— Defensive Player of the Year." *Football Digest*, April 2002.

"SI Players Poll." SI.com, October 24, 2006. Available online. URL: http://sportsillustrated.cnn.com/2006/players/10/24/ poll.1024/index.html.

Stellino, Vito. "Meet Urlacher's Trusty Sidekick—Rising Star: Rosevelt Colvin." *Football Digest*, February 2002.

Stevens, Richard. "Lobos Name Indoor Practice Facility Field in Honor of Brian Urlacher." Official Athletics of the University of New Mexico, June 24, 2009. Available online. URL: http://www.golobos.com/sports/m-footbl/spec-rel/062409aaa.html#.

"Urlacher Has Proud Mama Bear Cheering His Chicago Dream." *Albuquerque Tribune*, April 18, 2000. Available online. URL: http://www.abqtrib.com/news/2000/apr/18/urlacher-has-proud-mama-bear-cheering-his-chicago-/.

"Urlacher Sues over Autograph Contract Termination." *Sports Collectors Daily*, September 18, 2009. Available online. URL: http://www.sportscollectorsdaily.com/latest-sports-collecting-news/urlacher-sues-over-autograph-contract-termination.html.

Waddle, Brian. "Urlacher Tries to Forget Paris." *Bear Report*, September 24, 2003.

Warmbir, Steve. "Urlacher Pays for Dad Days." *Chicago Sun-Times*, October 10, 2006.

———. "Colts 29, Bears 17." Yahoo! Sports, February 5, 2007. Available online. URL: http://sports.yahoo.com/nfl/recap?gid=20070204003.

Wilner, Barry. "Defense Helps Bears Shuffle Off to Miami." Associated Press, January 22, 2007.

Zimmerman, Jason. "ESPN's Best NFL Players of Last 10 Years: Three Bears Players Named to All-Decade Team." Orato, June 28, 2009. Available online. URL: http://www.orato.com/sports/espns-best-nfl-players-of-last-10-years.

FURTHER READING

BOOKS

McDonough, Will. *The NFL Century: The Complete Story of the National Football League, 1920–2000*. New York: Smithmark, 1999.

Oriard, Michael. *Brand NFL: Making and Selling America's Favorite Sport*. Chapel Hill: University of North Carolina Press, 2007.

Palmer, Pete, et al. *The ESPN Pro Football Encyclopedia*, 2nd ed. New York: Sterling, 2007.

Stewart, Mark. *The Chicago Bears*. Chicago: Norwood House, 2007.

Taylor, Roy. *Chicago Bears History*. Mount Pleasant, S.C.: Arcadia Publishing, 2004.

Yost, Mark. *Tailgating, Sacks, and Salary Caps: How the NFL Became the Most Successful Sports League in History*. Chicago: Kaplan, 2006.

WEB SITES

Chicago Bears History
http://www.bearshistory.com/source/home.aspx

Chicago Bears Official Web Site
http://www.chicagobears.com/index.html

National Football League
http://www.nfl.com/

Pro Football Hall of Fame
http://www.profootballhof.com/

PICTURE CREDITS

INDEX

123

ABOUT THE AUTHOR

JON STERNGASS is the author of *First Resorts: Pursuing Pleasure at Saratoga Springs, Newport, and Coney Island* (Johns Hopkins University Press, 2001). He currently is a freelance writer specializing in children's nonfiction books; his most recent works are a biography of Crazy Horse and a book about the controversy over steroids use. Born and raised in Brooklyn, Jon Sterngass has a BA in history from Franklin and Marshall College, an MA in medieval history from the University of Wisconsin-Milwaukee, and a Ph.D in American history from City University of New York. He has resided in Saratoga Springs, New York, for 16 years with his wife, Karen Weltman, and sons Eli (17) and Aaron (14). He idolized Tommy Nobis and Willie Lanier as a kid and fancies himself a connoisseur of NFL middle linebackers.